80/20 ENDURANCE

The Complete System for High-Performance Coaching

MATT FITZGERALD

PUBLISHING

This book is dedicated to the many coaches whose commitment to their craft has developed the system of best practices from which we all benefit.

———

 PUBLISHING

80/20 Publishing, LLC
1073 Oberland Drive
Midway, UT 84049
www.8020books.com

Library of Congress Control Number: 2022950814
ISBN 979-8-9853980-2-1 (paperback)
ISBN 979-8-9853980-3-8 (e-book)

Cover and interior design: Vicki Hopewell
Cover photo: Jason Lehrbaum

Contents

Introduction

In 1997, a young exercise physiologist named Stephen Seiler moved from central Texas to southern Norway to take a job at the University of Agder. Among the responsibilities Seiler was given in his new role was that of performing fitness tests on the area's many elite cross-country skiers, who recorded some of the highest VO_2max scores he'd ever seen.

Imagine his surprise when, while running on the forested trails surrounding the university, Seiler saw these same athletes pause their own runs to walk up the steeper hills. He knew better than anyone how fit they were, yet Seiler himself never walked up the same hills. So why did they?

It was Inge Bråten, Norway's premier cross-country ski coach, who eventually supplied the answer. The walking thing, he said, was all about keeping workouts that were intended to target low intensity from creeping into moderate intensity, a zone that, in Bråten's experience, offered too little benefit at too great a cost. Hearing this explanation, Seiler recalled a study he'd read on the training practices of elite Kenyan distance runners, who evidently did most of their running at low intensity and most of the rest at high intensity, spending little time in the moderate-intensity range, just like Norway's top cross-country skiers.

Coincidence? Maybe, maybe not. But one thing was certain: Nothing that Seiler had ever learned through the kinds of controlled experiments he conducted in exercise science laboratories suggested that endurance athletes should balance their training intensities in the way these elite performers did. "I realized," Seiler recalled of this moment in a 2019 TEDx Talk, "I was going to have to leave the comfort of the laboratory and study elite athletes in *their* laboratories."

Convergent evolution in elite endurance sports

True to his promise, Seiler spent the next several years reviewing training data collected from elite endurance athletes across the world in sports ranging from cycling to rowing. What he discovered was that, almost universally, these athletes did about 80 percent of their training at low intensity and the remaining 20 percent at moderate to high intensity. But they hadn't always. Historical data showed that past generations of elite endurance athletes experimented with a variety of different intensity balances before settling on the 80/20 split seen today.

Biologists use the term *convergent evolution* to refer to a phenomenon whereby a particular biological feature evolves independently in multiple populations. Whenever a single, optimal solution exists to a problem that threatens the survival of living organisms, convergent evolution is expected to occur. The so-called camera eye is an often-cited example. This familiar visual organ represents the optimal biological solution to the problem of spatial orientation in animals, and for this reason it evolved independently in more than fifty species, including our own ancestors.

In the case of endurance training, an 80/20 intensity balance appears to be optimal for fitness and performance, and that's why top athletes in every major endurance discipline and in all parts of the world converged on this particular training method. In an influential 2009 paper, Seiler wrote, "In today's performance environment, where promising athletes have essentially unlimited time to train, all [elite] athletes train a lot and are highly motivated to optimize the training process. Training ideas that sound good but don't work in practice will fade away."

For convergent evolution itself to work, a high level of selection pressure must exist, meaning the price of failure must be steep. For living species, the price of failure to adapt is extinction, while for elite endurance athletes it is unemployment. When elite athletes fail to keep up with the latest training innovations, they may soon find themselves out of a job. But as motivated as most recreational endurance athletes are to improve, adopting and applying the very best available training methods is not the do-or-die matter it is for the pros. Hence, Seiler and his fellow researchers weren't terribly surprised when they learned that recreational endurance athletes train very differently from the pros, typically spending 30 to 50 percent of their weekly training time at *moderate* intensity. What if these everyday athletes adopted the same 80/20 intensity balance used by the elites?

Well, now we know: Controlled studies have found that athletes of all ability levels get faster when they slow down on their easy days. With few exceptions, cyclists, runners, and others who shift to an 80/20 intensity balance and stick with it can expect to improve to a far greater degree than they ever did with their habitual, mostly moderate training approach.

In hindsight, it's tempting to identify Seiler's discovery of the 80/20 rule of intensity balance as his single greatest contribution to endurance sports training. But it isn't. His most important insight is much broader, encompassing every aspect of endurance training methodology, not just intensity balance. What Seiler realized when he observed the world's best athletes voluntarily walking up hills during training runs was this: *Elite athletes know what the heck they're doing.* Until that moment, Seiler had assumed, like most exercise scientists, that laboratory experiments were the most reliable source of information about how to train for endurance. But he now saw that the real-world experiment engaged in by high-performing athletes day-in and day-out in training camps all over the world was far more valuable.

In our science-driven modern reality, we tend to think of formal experiments as being more rigorous than real-world trial and error, but where endurance training is concerned, the opposite is true. Given enough time, enough participants, and enough selection pressure, trial and error is almost guaranteed to find the best solution to many practical problems. This is why data scientists use genetic algorithms—a form of computer-based trial and error—to solve problems such as managing runway traffic at airports. And it is also why specific methods like the 80/20 intensity balance are practiced universally among the elites, and why controlled studies confirm that, sure enough, these methods are more effective than the alternatives. And not just for the elites, but for everyone.

A better training method for all athletes

In 2014, I authored a book titled *80/20 Running*, which aimed to bring Seiler's discovery to the masses. After a slow start, it became a surprise bestseller, spreading by word of mouth as athletes tried the method it taught, got good results, and encouraged others to do the same. Two years later, I partnered with triathlon coach David Warden to write a follow-up book called *80/20 Triathlon* (the foreword to which was written by none other than Dr. Stephen Seiler) and to launch 80/20 Endurance, an online resource dedicated to making elite training methods available to everyone. As with the first book, early adopters of these new offerings achieved performance breakthroughs and subsequently shared their "secret" with others, who did the same, leading to exponential growth.

As the 80/20 Endurance training method continues to spread globally, interest in coaching the method has grown commensurately. This book was written to meet a rising demand from current and aspiring coaches who wish to train athletes the 80/20 way, either professionally or casually. It serves as a companion piece to the online 80/20 Endurance Coach Certification course, which you can learn more about at https://learning.8020endurance .com. But what exactly is the 80/20 way? Is it all about intensity balance?

It is not. Rather, it is a complete training system based on Stephen Seiler's core insight that the methods used broadly by the world's best endurance athletes are the most effective methods for all athletes. It is, in short, a "best practices" approach to training endurance athletes. While the 80/20 intensity balance may be the most important of these practices, it is not the only one. If the only thing you knew about endurance training was that athletes should spend about 80 percent of their time at low intensity and the remaining 20 percent at moderate to high intensity, you would not be an effective coach. The goal of this book is to impart *all* of the knowledge you will need to be an effective endurance coach, and there's a whole lot more to coaching than helping athletes avoid the common mistake of spending too much time at moderate intensity.

Even absolute beginners should be encouraged to emulate the professionals in their training—not in every detail, of course, but certainly in the fundamentals. There is no barrier to doing so. The 80/20 approach is both accessible and gentler on the body than the 50/50 training most nonelite athletes do. In this sense, our efforts to spread the message of 80/20 training to athletes everywhere can be regarded as a mission to democratize the best practices of elite athletes in endurance training. Why should only the most gifted athletes have access to the most effective training methods?

A better methodology for coaches

Similarly, this book is part of a mission to democratize endurance coaching. We believe that anyone can coach endurance athletes effectively if they truly want to. Helping athletes reach their potential doesn't require an encyclopedic knowledge of exercise science or years of experience as a high-level athlete. Like the 80/20 method itself, good coaching is simple. It depends not so much on knowledge or experience as on a number of core principles that are easy to absorb. No person who feels called to coach endurance athletes should hesitate to heed this call out of fear that they don't have what it takes. Make no mistake: coaching is challenging work, yet success is nearly automatic for those who stay true to the core principles. *80/20 Endurance* is focused on teaching these core principles, along with the foundational knowledge required to coach endurance athletes toward their goals.

Not a coach yet? That's okay. Most of the material in the book applies to self-coached athletes as much as it does to those who coach others. Throughout the twelve chapters that follow, we will address the reader as "coach," but by no means do we mean to exclude self-coached athletes. Whether you intend to apply what you learn to other athletes or only to your own training, the knowledge you gain here will be of value.

The layout is straightforward. Chapter 1 offers a broad overview of the 80/20 approach to coaching endurance. The next four chapters address the rudiments of endurance training, including intensity, volume, workout types, and periodization. The following chapters will teach you how to monitor and adjust athletes' training, apply the 80/20 approach to different sport types, oversee strength and mobility training, and guide athletes through competition.

As any experienced coach knows, helping athletes regulate their thoughts and emotions in productive ways is a big part of the job, and Chapter 10 delivers pragmatic guidance on this important topic. The next two chapters discuss the ethical and business aspects of coaching, and at the back of the book you'll find a rigorously curated list of resources for furthering your coaching education. Whether your goal is to become a certified 80/20 Endurance coach or just to learn, we encourage you to take full advantage of these resources and cultivate a deeper understanding of endurance coaching. We promise you won't regret the investment.

Coaching endurance athletes is every bit as rewarding as it is challenging. If you already have some coaching experience, you know this, and if you're at the beginning of your coaching journey, you're about to find out. Endurance sports are not your typical hobby; they demand a lot from participants, even those who are not competitive. Most endurance athletes don't just *like* their chosen sport, they *love* it, finding deep personal meaning in their athletic journey. Their goals are extremely important to them, and when they achieve these goals they are pleased beyond measure, profoundly grateful to those who helped along the way. The job of the endurance coach is just that—to help athletes achieve their goals. Gratitude is the greatest reward that coaches receive for doing their job, not only in moments of glory but throughout the journey. Congratulations on embarking on your own journey—you've made an excellent choice!

Principles of Endurance Training

⟋ The core principles of endurance training equip coaches to make good training decisions for athletes despite whatever remains unknown.

⟋ Effective endurance training is purposeful, balanced, specific to the demands of racing, progressive, and cyclical.

⟋ Successful endurance coaches tailor an athlete's training to the individual athlete and continuously adapt training based on the athlete's response. They also make a consistent effort to maximize the athlete's enjoyment of the training process.

Coaching endurance athletes is largely a matter of helping them determine what to do now, what to do next, and what to do in the future. Each of these decisions is constrained by available information. The more information you have, the more your options narrow, and the easier your decisions become. In a situation where you had no information—if you knew nothing at all about the athlete or about endurance training in general—it would be impossible to make any planning decisions with confidence.

Fortunately, you will never find yourself in this position. You will always have some information that constrains your options and enables you to help the athlete determine how to proceed in their training. The most important piece of information you can have is the athlete's immediate goal, which in most cases is to get as fit as possible for their next race. Keeping this goal in mind when making planning decisions will narrow your options, eliminating ones that aren't consistent with this goal.

The options for what to do with a given athlete's training are further constrained by your knowledge of endurance training, of the athlete, and of the immediate situation. Again, the more information you have, the fewer options remain, such that in a state of perfect information, where you know absolutely everything needed to make the decision, only one option will remain. The decision is effectively made for you.

For better or worse, having access to perfect information is just as rare as having no information at all. Because of this, coaches must rely on things over and above available information to make a final call on how to proceed. Chief among these other things are the *core principles of endurance training*: purpose, balance, specificity, progression, cyclicality, adaptivity, individualization, and enjoyment.

Together, these eight principles form a decision-making logic that essentially fills the gap left open by incomplete information. Although you will never know everything you would need to know to deduce the right decision on behalf of an individual athlete in a particular situation, you can still make decisions with a high degree of confidence if you understand these principles. The first step in becoming an effective endurance coach, therefore, is learning these fundamental principles. The discussion that follows will establish a big-picture view of endurance coaching. Subsequent chapters will fill in the details, highlighting specific applications of each principle as it occurs.

Purpose → Performance drives endurance training.

Purpose distinguishes training from exercise. A person who swims for the purpose of living longer is exercising, not training, as is a person who rides a mountain bike to commune with nature and a person who runs for the purpose of losing weight. Performance is the defining purpose of endurance training. It's a key distinction because with this shift in purpose comes a shift in approach.

Health and fitness goals such as weight management and longevity are open-ended. A nonathlete exerciser can repeat the same workout routine year-round and meet their goal in an ongoing way. With athletes, it's different. To maximize their performance in races and other events, they must evolve their workout routine in a way that increases their fitness as much as possible before their next event. Hence, whereas exercise tends to be static in nature, sufficing to maintain certain desired benefits, training is directional, aiming to maximize the specific benefits of fitness and performance.

Although performance is the defining purpose of endurance training, it is not the only purpose. Athletes can't just keep getting fitter and fitter all the time, so there are times when the primary purpose of workouts might be recovery or even fun, such as when a competitive runner takes a break from running to cross-country ski in winter. Other purposes that athletes might pursue when not actively building fitness for an event include rehabilitating an injury or building strength. What's most important from a coaching perspective is that you identify a clear, appropriate purpose for an athlete's training at all times. This purpose should also be communicated to the athlete so they can do their part to fulfill it.

Goals play an important role in relation to the purpose principle. In a sense, they encode the purpose of a training period. For example, if an athlete's goal is to make the podium in their next "A" race, preparing the athlete to achieve this goal becomes the purpose of the training leading up to the race. We will have much to say on the topic of goal setting in the chapters ahead.

Balance → Adhere to an 80/20 intensity balance.

Endurance training is a balancing act. For 80/20 coaches, intensity balance is the most obvious consideration. Making sure your athletes spend about 80 percent of their training time at low intensity and 20 percent at moderate to high intensity is key. Almost as important, though, is guiding them toward balancing harder and easier training sessions within the week, as well as heavier and lighter workloads from week to week.

To better understand the value of balancing specific training stimuli, let's say you're coaching a runner who is training for a marathon that will take place on a course with a few rolling hills. Among the specific stimuli this athlete will need to experience in training in order to perform their best on race day are long endurance runs, high-intensity hill repetitions, and marathon-pace runs. But these sessions don't need to be done with equal frequency. A balance of roughly one long endurance run every week, one high-intensity hill repetitions workout every two to three weeks, and two to three marathon-pace runs sprinkled into the final six to eight weeks of the training cycle should do the trick. Factors to consider in determining the balance of different training stimuli include the nature of the athlete's goal event, where the athlete is in the training cycle (priorities will evolve as fitness increases and race day draws nearer), and how much of each individual stimulus is needed to maximize its potential contribution to overall performance.

Consideration should also be given to an athlete's training/life balance. Even a professional endurance athlete has a life outside of the sport that impacts their training. As a coach, you want to be aware of what's going on in the life of each athlete. An athlete has only one "fuel tank" to draw from when it comes to finding energy for a significant undertaking, whether it be a challenging swim set or a work project with a tight deadline. Likewise, stressors of every kind, from exhausting tempo rides to sick children, impact an athlete's tolerance for other stressors. No matter how important training is to an athlete, never lose sight of the fact that, in the long run, they will make more progress if a proper balance is maintained between their training and the rest of their life.

Specificity ⇢ Train the athlete for the demands of the event.

Fitness looks different depending on the goal. The type of fitness a powerlifter needs to compete successfully in powerlifting tournaments, for example, is vastly different from the type of fitness an ultra-endurance cyclist needs to complete multiday races. Likewise, at a more nuanced level, the type of fitness a runner requires to excel at the marathon distance is a bit different from the type of fitness a runner needs to excel at the 1500-meter distance.

It is essential that you train your athletes in a manner that equips them with the specific type of fitness they need for their next important race. Returning to the example just given, the 1500-meter event demands greater ***anaerobic capacity*** than the marathon, which in turn demands greater fat-burning capacity than the metric mile. Hence, if you're training a runner for the shorter of these events, you'll want to place greater emphasis on high-intensity intervals, which improve anaerobic capacity, and less emphasis on long runs, which improve fat-burning capacity, than if you're training the same runner for the longer distance.

The principle of specificity extends only so far, however. A 1500-meter runner won't get very far doing all of their training at race pace, nor will a marathoner attain optimal fitness by running 42.2 kilometers every day. Yes, a 1500-meter runner needs more anaerobic capacity and less fat-burning capacity than a marathoner, but a 1500-meter runner still needs a high fat-burning capacity, and a marathon runner needs some anaerobic development. Furthermore, both runners need other things besides anaerobic capacity and fat-burning capacity. Running is running, after all, so for the most part, the training program of a 1500-meter runner should look quite similar to that of a marathon runner. The same components will factor into two different programs, only the proportions will differ. In short, while specificity is important, a little specificity goes a long way.

To underscore this point, observational studies have found that elite middle-distance runners and elite long-distance runners adhere to an 80/20 intensity balance, as do short-course and long-course specialists in other endurance disciplines. Further evidence shows that optimal fitness for longer race distances is similar to optimal fitness for shorter distances comes from individual examples of elite endurance athletes who have won major championships at disparate distances on the strength of a single training program. One such example is Karen Smyers, an American triathlete who won the 1995 ITU World Championship, an Olympic-distance event, five weeks after she won the much longer Ironman World Championship. Another example is Dutch runner Sifan Hassan, who won the 2019 IAAF Outdoor Championships 1500m one week after she won the 10,000m event at the same meet. If Ironman fitness weren't mostly the same thing as Olympic-distance triathlon fitness, and if 10,000-meter fitness did not overlap significantly with 1500-meter fitness, these things couldn't have happened.

The principle of specificity applies not only to preparing for races of different distances but also to preparing for specific race conditions. Indeed, for athletes who compete in highly challenging environments, conditions-specific preparation should be prioritized above other forms of race-specific preparation. A limited amount of cycling at 40K time-trial power, for example, will suffice to prepare an athlete for optimal performance in a 40K cycling time trial. But a single training run on a technical mountain trail will not prepare a runner for optimal performance in a sky race. Any runner who attempted to complete a sky race after having completed just one training run on terrain similar to that of the race course would pay a heavy price, developing premature soreness and fatigue in muscles that aren't tested the same way on less challenging terrain.

In addition to terrain and topography, climate, weather, and elevation must also be considered in applying the principle of specificity to training. An athlete who lives at high elevation should, if possible, do a few key workouts at a lower elevation to get used to the speed that is likely to be attainable for them in an upcoming sea-level race. Similarly, an athlete preparing for a race that is likely to take place in extreme heat should do some training in a hot environment, outdoors if feasible.

In summary, specificity in training is not to be overlooked by a coach, nor should it be overemphasized.

Progression → Volume and intensity progress fitness.

Progression is probably the most intuitive endurance training principle. Whereas other, less intuitive, principles were discovered through trial and error, athletes have always understood that they must do a little before they can do a lot, and that's progression in a nutshell. More than twenty-six centuries ago, Milo of Croton developed the strength that carried him to six Olympic wrestling titles by lifting a calf off the ground every day until it grew into an adult bull. Each time Milo raised the animal, it was slightly heavier, and he got a little stronger. There is no clearer demonstration of the progression principle.

In endurance training, progression is achieved through the manipulation of two key variables: volume and intensity. Volume, of course, is the amount of training an athlete does, while intensity is how hard the athlete is working in relation to their limit. The combination of these two variables is referred to as *training load*. To achieve progression in their training, endurance athletes must increase their training load, either by training more, training at a higher intensity, or both.

Various metrics are used to quantify training load. The best known among these is Banister's training impulse (TRIMP), which uses time and heart-rate data to calculate a stress score for individual workouts. The greater the stress score, the larger the anticipated fitness-boosting effect of the workout. The formula used to calculate TRIMP scores is fairly complex because the relationship between intensity and physiological stress is nonlinear. At higher intensities, each incremental uptick in effort adds more stress than the last. So a 45-minute workout completed at a steady heart rate of 151 bpm (beats per minute) is significantly less stressful to the body than a 45-minute workout that includes several one-minute sprints peaking at a heart rate of 180 bpm yet still results in the same average heart rate. This difference will be reflected in TRIMP scores for the two workouts.

Things get even more complicated when you try to measure cumulative training loads over time. This is because individual workouts generate both fatigue and fitness. Fatigue manifests immediately and is processed by the body over a period of days, whereas fitness is gained and lost on a longer time scale. The metric that is most commonly used to quantify cumulative training fatigue is *acute training load* (ATL), which is calculated as a rolling average of training stress imposed on the athlete over the preceding week. Fitness is commonly quantified as chronic training load (CTL), which is calculated as the rolling average of training stress imposed on the athlete over the preceding four to six weeks. Online platforms, including TrainingPeaks®, perform these calculations automatically, but it takes active effort on the part of the coach to maintain the reliability of these numbers. For example, the TrainingPeaks equivalent of TRIMP is *training stress score* (TSS). To generate an accurate TSS for a given workout, TrainingPeaks uses the athlete's current lactate threshold heart rate, pace, or power, so it's important that this information be kept up to date.

While useful, TRIMP, TSS, and other such metrics are not essential to measuring and regulating training loads. As an 80/20 Endurance coach, you can monitor and control training loads effectively in other ways. One advantage of the 80/20 system is that the distribution of intensities is held fairly constant, allowing coaches to keep abreast of an athlete's training load by focusing mainly on *volume*, measured in either time or distance.

Subjective assessments of training load are also useful. In fact, they are the only load measure that truly is indispensable. Research has demonstrated that perceptions and feelings such as fatigue, lack of enjoyment, and loss of motivation are among the most reliable indicators of nonfunctional *overreaching* (or training beyond one's capacity to recover and adapt). An athlete who feels as though they are close to the limit of their training load tolerance is almost certainly right, regardless of what their ATL and CTL numbers are at the time. The single most important piece of information you can collect from an athlete after they've completed a workout is how it felt to them. Consistently monitoring how your athletes feel during the training process will enable you to identify and quickly react to possible nonfunctional overreaching, averting the worst consequences.

Speaking of overreaching, it should be noted that it is not always necessary to increase an athlete's training load to boost their fitness level. Athletes who are currently training too much or too intensely will begin to feel fitter and perform better if their training load is appropriately reduced, allowing them to emerge from a state of overreaching. The most common scenario is the so-called moderate-intensity rut, where the athlete is spending too much time at moderate intensity and not enough time at low intensity. At any given training load, an 80/20 balance produces less fatigue than a more aggressive intensity distribution, allowing athletes to reach higher fitness levels without overreaching.

Keep in mind also that, as stated above, there are many different kinds of fitness. It's impossible to make apples-to-apples comparisons between the fitness level of athletes training for different events. Yet the metrics commonly used to quantify endurance fitness try to do just that. In particular, these metrics tend to be biased toward volume. Going back to our earlier example, elite marathon runners necessarily train at higher volumes than elite 1500-meter runners, so their training loads are greater. Does this mean they're fitter? Not really. It's more accurate to say that elite marathoners are fitter for marathons and elite 1500-meter runners are fitter for 1500-meter races. Coaches who focus on metrics like TRIMP and CTL and forget about the specificity of fitness are prone to fall short of optimizing the event-specific fitness of their athletes. There are no medals awarded for TRIMP or CTL scores.

Another nuance of training loads that is important to understand is that athletes are changed by their training. For this reason, it is entirely possible for an athlete to repeat the same training program and attain a higher level of competitive performance at the end of the second cycle than they did at the end of the first. By virtue of having gone through the program once, the athlete starts the second cycle with a slightly different body, so it's not really the same program, even though the training load is the same.

Elite athletes depend on this non-repeatability factor to make progress over the course of their careers. Most elite endurance athletes reach the limit of their individual training load tolerance by their mid-twenties, yet they often continue to improve for many years thereafter through sheer consistency. These athletes also tend to make small refinements to their personal training formula in accordance with the principle of individualization, which we will discuss shortly. Even recreational athletes who never train hard enough to reach their own maximal training load tolerance (perhaps due to time constraints) can achieve long-term progress in this manner.

Cyclicality → Cycle progression and recovery for adaptation.

We have just seen that progressive endurance training achieves its fundamental objective of improving fitness. Simply put, fitness increases when training load increases, except in cases where an athlete is already training too much or too intensely. But this doesn't mean the training load can or should increase continuously. Again, the reason is that training produces not only fitness but also fatigue, which accumulates more rapidly. An athlete who tries to continuously increase their training load will soon enter a state of nonfunctional overreaching, where the body is no longer able to adapt to the training.

This is why well-coached endurance athletes train in cycles, where an overall pattern of progression is punctuated by periods of reduced training that allow the athlete to catch up on recovery. This needs to happen on three distinct timescales. The shortest cycles are known as *microcycles*, which usually align with seven-day calendar weeks. Athletes at all levels of fitness must include at least one rest day or light training day within the week to avoid overreaching. *Mesocycles* (also called step cycles) are somewhat longer, lasting three to four weeks, which is about as long as athletes can go before needing a somewhat deeper recovery comprising several days to a week with a reduced training load. The longest and most flexible cycles are *macrocycles*, which last a few months, terminating at the point where the athlete reaches a maximal training load tolerance. To get any fitter, the athlete will need to take a break from progressive training and then start a fresh macrocycle. The athletic development achieved through the previous macrocycle is then leveraged to attain a greater peak training load, hence a higher level of fitness.

Not all overreaching is nonfunctional. Indeed, the whole point of training in cycles is to bring about a state of **functional overreaching**, which occurs when the athlete is training at a level that, although not sustainable, is also not beyond their capacity to beneficially adapt. As long as it is not taken too far, this type of overreaching yields greater fitness than is attainable through a sustainable workload, and it is the rest days, recovery weeks, and "off-season" breaks within the various cycles that keep functional overreaching from becoming nonfunctional.

A cyclical approach to endurance training has an emotional component as well. Effective training requires a high level of motivation. Because of this, and because hard training demands a significant commitment of time and energy and a lot of personal sacrifice, peak training loads are both physically and emotionally unsustainable.

Adaptivity → Continually adjust training based on the response.

Training outcomes are inherently unpredictable. Coaches never know exactly how an athlete will respond to the training prescribed, and the actual results seldom match the expected results in every detail. Sometimes the gap between expectation and reality is small, other times not so small. For example, an athlete might find the training harder than you thought they would, or a certain component of an athlete's fitness will improve more slowly than you anticipated. Surprises like these don't constitute coaching errors because they aren't entirely preventable. What does constitute a coaching error is failing to adapt appropriately. That might mean dialing back the training load of an athlete who's feeling overwhelmed, trying a different approach to develop a component of fitness that's coming along more slowly than you'd like, or making another reasonable adjustment.

If training outcomes were fully predictable, then planning would be a one-and-done undertaking for coaches. At the start of a new training cycle, the coach would create a plan for the complete cycle, the athlete would execute the plan to the letter, and everyone would live happily ever after. Because training outcomes are in fact unpredictable, the planning process must be continuous, a matter of revising the original plan weekly or even daily—in other words, as often as necessary—in response to actual outcomes. This is the principle of adaptivity in a nutshell.

The unpredictability of training outcomes should not be taken as an excuse to train by the seat of one's pants. While adaptive training requires a great deal of flexibility from both the coach and the athlete, it's still important to have an overarching plan for training. This gives you something to reference training outcomes against—a roadmap showing where you want to take the athlete and the straightest path to that destination. The inevitable surprises that occur in training are like accidental detours that require the coach to identify the straightest path to the destination from where the athlete is *now*, rather than from where the athlete was expected to be at this point before the journey began.

Individualization → Continually adapt training to the individual.

The principle of individualization overlaps with that of adaptivity. If every athlete were the same, then planning workouts in a provisional way and adjusting them in response to disparities between expectation and reality would be necessary for one reason only, which is the inherent unpredictability of training outcomes. But because each athlete is unique, part of the process is figuring out (i.e., learning) the individual athlete, a process that never ends, for in addition to being unique, each athlete is also continuously changing. If you are open to this process in the same way you're open to the inherent unpredictability of endurance training, you will become a better and better coach to each individual athlete the longer you work with them.

The process of *individualization* should begin before the first workout is prescribed. Step one in working with any new athlete is information gathering. You'll want to learn the athlete's age, sex, athletic history, current fitness level, goals, injury history, training environment, life schedule, and training preferences. Appendix A presents a (triathlete-specific) sample athlete intake questionnaire that can be used for this purpose. This information will enable you to tailor the athlete's initial training in ways that make it superior to a cookie-cutter plan. But if the process unfolds as it should, the training you prescribe for this same athlete one year later will look a lot different in specific ways that reflect what you've learned about them in that time.

There are many dimensions to athletic individuality. Some athletes crush their speed work yet struggle in long endurance sessions. Some athletes respond more quickly than others to threshold training, or any other type of training stimulus you can name. Some athletes can handle larger amounts of a particular training stimulus. Some need more time to recover from a certain type of workout. Some athletes are predisposed to tendon injuries, muscle strains, or stress fractures, and still others are highly resistant to injury in general.

You get the idea. Our goal here is not to exhaustively list all the ways athletes differ from one another and how that may impact coaching them, but rather, the point we're trying to make is that it's a very long list with lots of subtleties. The best way to address this complex reality is simply to pay attention and be receptive to new discoveries. Don't be afraid to develop hypotheses and test them in low-risk ways. For example, you might have a hunch that a particular athlete will better tolerate their current training load if you divide some of their daily training sessions into pairs of shorter, morning-and-afternoon sessions.

It's okay, and even advisable, to let your athlete know what you're doing in these situations. Explain to each new athlete right up front that it takes time for you or any coach to get a good feel for how to guide an individual athlete's training most effectively. This will set appropriate expectations and help the athlete understand the process.

Enjoyment → Maximize fitness and performance with enjoyment.

For too many coaches, enjoyment is an afterthought. It's not that they don't care whether their athletes are having fun; they just don't fully appreciate its impact. These coaches focus on prescribing workouts that maximize physical benefits and just sort of hope, or assume, the athlete will enjoy them. To a certain extent, this assumption is fair. All athletes enjoy improving, so a coach who focuses entirely on conditioning the body might see the implicit hope for athlete enjoyment realized in some measure.

The link between fitness and enjoyment flows in both directions, however. Athletes are human beings, not exercise machines. In endurance training, the body goes where the mind leads as much as the mind goes where the body leads. If there were a Hall of Fame for endurance coaches, it would be dominated by coaches who had a special gift for keeping their athletes motivated, not by technical savants. Research has demonstrated that enjoyment is strongly correlated with performance in individual workouts and competitions and that it also predicts improvement over time. Even if you cared only about the fitness and performance of your athletes and not at all about how they experience the training process, you would still want to prioritize enjoyment for the sake of maximizing fitness and performance.

As a coach, you are not responsible for making your athletes like their sport. That's on them. But you should do what you can to enhance the fun factor as they go through the process. This begins with consistent monitoring of your athletes' enjoyment. Paying attention to their emotional response to training will not only let you know when there's a problem that needs to be addressed, but it will also teach you their preferences and aversions so you can plan future training accordingly. Athletes seek to fulfill one of three primary psychological needs through sports participation: affiliation, achievement, and ego. Affiliation seekers derive enjoyment from the social dimension of sport participation, achievement seekers from improvement, and ego seekers from recognition. Identifying what psychologically drives your athletes can help you craft a more enjoyable training experience.

Don't go too far in accommodating individual athlete preferences, however. Left to their own devices, many athletes avoid or give lip service to the elements of training they enjoy least. Part of your job is to get your athletes to embrace these elements. But there's more than one way to plan a week of training that will meet a given athlete's immediate physiological needs, so select the option you believe they'll enjoy most.

WHEN IN DOUBT, TRUST THE PRINCIPLES

As we have seen, uncertainty is inherent to endurance coaching. Even the most knowledgeable and experienced coaches have moments of uncertainty in guiding their athletes—decision points where they're just not sure what the right move is. A thorough understanding of the core principles of endurance training is your best insurance in these moments. Whenever you find yourself in a state of doubt about what to do with an athlete, go back to the principles of purpose, balance, specificity, progression, cyclicality, adaptivity, individualization, and enjoyment, and make the decision that is most consistent with the most relevant principle(s). Doing so won't guarantee that you always make the right call, but it will ensure you make the right call more often than not.

Training Intensities and Workout Types

✓ Intensity is the most important variable in endurance training because it determines the primary effect of any given workout on an athlete's fitness.

✓ The first ventilatory threshold, which marks the boundary between low intensity and moderate intensity, is key to balancing intensity. Workouts intended to target low intensity must take place below this threshold to achieve their desired effect.

✓ It is possible to train any athlete effectively with a limited set of basic workouts targeting low, moderate, and high intensity.

W orkouts are the fundamental building blocks of endurance training. They come in many different types, each defined by a specific purpose (*principle of purpose*). The three main variables that endurance coaches manipulate in designing workouts are:

1

intensity, or how
hard the athlete
is working in relation
to their limit;

2

duration,
or distance; and

3

structure, or how
the workout is divided
into segments of
different intensities
and lengths.

Of these, ***intensity*** is primary in that it determines the purpose, duration/distance, and structure of the workout. For example, VO_2max intensity corresponds to an effort that the average trained athlete can sustain for roughly six minutes. The benefits of training at or near this intensity are increased aerobic capacity, better fatigue resistance at higher exercise intensities, and increased tolerance for the discomfort associated with sustained high-intensity efforts. Workouts targeting this intensity are almost always structured as sets of high-intensity intervals separated by brief periods of active recovery. This structure maximizes the time that athletes are able to spend at or near the targeted intensity without overtaxing themselves. Even the fittest athletes can only handle so many VO_2max intervals, however, so these workouts tend to be shorter than many other workout types.

Like all of the best practices in endurance training, the workout types that high-performing endurance athletes use today came about through a long-term, collective process of trial and error. Each generation of elite athletes, having inherited a collection of workouts from their predecessors, experimented with various permutations of these formats, assessed the results, retained formats that seemed to yield good results, and discarded those that didn't. They then passed down a refined collection of workouts to the next generation. For example, the deep-sand runs favored by the Olympians of ancient Greece have long since fallen into disuse, whereas the interval training methods pioneered by German track coach Woldemar Gerschler in the 1930s remain widely practiced.

This evolutionary process continues today. There's really no limit to the number of ways an endurance training session can be modified to offer something that hasn't been tried before. Recent innovations have come from exercise scientists searching for ways to tweak existing workout designs to increase their effectiveness. One example is decreasing intervals, which consist of high-intensity segments that decrease in duration as the session progresses, as do the active recovery periods between them. In testing, the inventors of this workout found that cyclists were able to accumulate more total time at or near VO_2max than they did in more traditional interval sets involving segments of fixed duration. What's more, they did so without actually feeling that they'd worked any harder. In short, this new format seemed to offer more potential benefit at equal cost to the athlete compared to traditional designs.

Does this mean descending intervals are superior to older formats that have survived the test of time? Not exactly. There is no single workout, new or old, that every athlete must do to realize their full potential. If there were, we would see certain workouts practiced the same way by elite endurance athletes everywhere. Even something as seemingly universal as the good old-fashioned easy run isn't practiced the same way in all places. In Ethiopia, for example, elite runners rarely complete easy runs entirely at low intensity, as most runners elsewhere do. Instead, they ratchet up their pace toward the end of the run, often finishing at a full sprint.

Science is wonderful, but as coaches we mustn't extract broad conclusions from isolated experiments. The laboratory is not the real world, and the tests that are done in that artificially simplified environment have limited relevance to the messy, sprawling environments that athletes live, train, and compete in. The coach who tunes out science completely does so at their peril, but real-world evidence should have the deciding vote.

There's a phenomenon known as novelty bias that causes some athletes and coaches to assume that newer and more exotic workout formats are better than older and more basic formats. It may be true that veteran athletes who have already realized close to 100 percent of their innate potential through a particular repertoire of workouts will benefit from incorporating more sophisticated formats into their training, but some of the world's most successful endurance athletes prefer to keep their workouts quite simple. This is good news for less experienced coaches because it means they don't need to invest a lot of time and energy into getting comfortable with a huge variety of complex workout formats to train athletes effectively.

In an effort to be inclusive and as helpful as possible, we've chosen to tightly focus the following discussion of training intensities and workout types. Our objective is to distinguish what's important to know about intensity from what isn't and to define a set of basic building blocks that will allow a coach to practice the 80/20 Endurance training method with good results. All of the workouts that follow are included in the 80/20 Endurance workout library. Don't feel obligated to use these and only these workout designs in your coaching. Other, more complex workouts can be highly beneficial. Just remember they aren't essential, especially when you're getting started as an 80/20 Endurance coach.

Physiological Markers of Training Intensity

Exercise intensity is a complex subject. You could devote years to studying the underlying physiology of intensity and still fall short of fully demystifying it. As a coach, however, you only need to know a few things about intensity in order to manipulate this critical training variable effectively with your athletes.

The practice of dividing the full spectrum of exercise intensities into smaller segments, or zones, helps athletes perform different types of workouts correctly, ensuring they don't go too hard or too easy to fulfill a given workout's purpose. There are many different ways to split the intensity spectrum into zones. You might expect us to claim that the 80/20 Endurance zone scale (see Table 2.1, p. 21) is superior to all others, but we won't, because it isn't. While our zone scale is certainly better than some—such as those based on the discredited Karvonen formula for estimating maximum heart rate (subtracting the athlete's age from 220)—there are other zone scales that are equally useful. The better zone scales are anchored to specific physiological phenomena in a way that ensures workouts performed in each zone have the desired effect. Let's now have a look at physiology of intensity.

First Ventilatory Threshold

Where intensity is concerned, the phenomenon that matters above all else is the *first ventilatory threshold* (VT_1), which is the lower of two intensities at which an athlete's breathing rate spikes. Athletes often conflate zones and thresholds, but they are distinct. Whereas a zone is a range of intensities, a threshold is a specific intensity point. Thresholds are often, but not always, used to mark the boundaries (i.e., upper and lower limits) of intensity zones. This is the case with the first ventilatory threshold. In heart rate terms, the VT_1 falls between 77 and 81 percent of maximum heart rate for most athletes, and, in subjective terms, it corresponds to a perceived effort rating of 4 on a 1–10 scale. Notably, the first ventilatory threshold also corresponds to the highest work rate at which an athlete can comfortably carry on a conversation. Training above the VT_1 is significantly more stressful to the sympathetic nervous system than training below it. Of course, athletes will need to train above the VT_1, but they should be careful not to drift above this threshold in workouts that are intended to target low intensity. Most exercise scientists now regard the VT_1 as the true dividing line between low intensity and moderate intensity.

VO$_2$max

A second physiological threshold that is important in relation to exercise intensity is **VO$_2$max**, which is the intensity at which an athlete encounters the limit of their capacity to consume oxygen. Sometimes referred to as the aerobic engine, an athlete's VO_2max (measured as milliliters of oxygen consumed per kilogram of bodyweight per minute) can be compared to a vehicle's horsepower. There are three fundamental ways to increase endurance performance. One is to increase the size of the aerobic engine, or how fast the athlete can go at their metabolic limit. Another is to increase efficiency, enabling the athlete to sustain a higher percentage of their VO_2max over a given duration. And the third is to increase the athlete's range, or endurance, the equivalent of enlarging a vehicle's fuel tank, which allows the athlete to sustain a given output longer before reaching exhaustion.

As mentioned, in the typical trained endurance athlete, VO_2max intensity corresponds to the highest rate of energy expenditure that can be sustained for about six minutes. Training at or very near VO_2max is an especially powerful means of increasing **aerobic capacity**, or the body's ability to use inspired oxygen to generate muscle work. A properly designed and executed endurance training program will regularly feature workouts in which the athlete spends a fair amount of time working at or near VO_2max intensity.

Lactate Threshold

A third physiological threshold that matters in endurance training, though not as much as the two already discussed, is the **lactate threshold**. This is the intensity at which lactate, an intermediate product of aerobic metabolism in the muscles, begins to accumulate in the bloodstream. The typical trained endurance athlete can sustain this intensity for about one hour in race conditions. There was a time when most exercise scientists and many endurance coaches believed that training at this intensity was the most potent way to improve race performance. This belief was based on research demonstrating a strong correlation between race performance and the speed or power at which individual athletes hit their lactate threshold.

Just as novelty bias can factor into training decisions, here we have an example of measurement bias, or inflating the importance of the things we measure. Lactate threshold is easy to measure, and that is why exercise scientists became infatuated with it, but it's not the be-all and end-all of endurance training. Nevertheless, it remains worthwhile to do some training at or near lactate threshold intensity, and the various field tests used to estimate lactate threshold and the intensity zones derived from those results remain valid.

Second Ventilatory Threshold

Another intensity threshold that endurance coaches need to know and understand is the **second ventilatory threshold** (VT_2), which falls between 91 and 93 percent of maximum heart rate for the majority of athletes. Like the VT_1, the VT_2 is marked by an abrupt spike in the breathing rate, and it coincides almost perfectly with critical power (or critical velocity), which is the highest exercise intensity at which the body maintains a relatively stable metabolic state. This intensity is sustainable for 20 to 30 minutes in time-to-exhaustion tests.

The mechanisms that cause fatigue to occur at or below the VT_2 differ from those that bring about exhaustion when exercising above it. Hence, the specific effects of training above or below the VT_2 are distinct, as are the optimal workout formats for stimulating these effects. It's useful, therefore, to position the dividing line between moderate intensity and high intensity at the VT_2, as growing numbers of exercise scientists now do.

Functional Correlates

It's worth noting that physiological testing is required to pinpoint the first ventilatory threshold, the lactate threshold, and the second ventilatory threshold in individual athletes. Does this mean that physiological testing is needed to regulate intensity effectively in endurance training? It does not. Lots of elite endurance athletes reach the top of their sport with little or no help from physiological testing. It is possible to regulate intensity without the aid of an exercise laboratory by targeting the ***functional correlates*** of various physiological thresholds. A functional correlate is simply a performance standard or other practical limit that corresponds to a particular physiological threshold. These correlates can be used in training as proxies for physiological intensity targets, allowing things like power meters, heart rate monitors, and even subjective perceptions to take the place of blood lactate measurements and so forth.

The 80/20 Endurance zone scale aligns the boundaries between certain zones with specific functional correlates of physiological thresholds. You will recall that lactate threshold intensity corresponds to the highest output an athlete can sustain for approximately one hour. An athlete's average pace, power, or heart rate in a one-hour time trial is therefore a functional correlate of lactate threshold intensity. Better yet, there are simple field tests that can be done in place of a one-hour time trial that are proven to yield accurate lactate threshold estimates. For example, a cyclist can perform a 20-minute time trial and multiply

TABLE 2.1 **THE 80/20 ENDURANCE ZONE SCALE**

ZONE	FUNCTIONAL DEFINITION	PHYSIOLOGICAL CORRELATE
1	Sustainable indefinitely	- - -
2	Upper limit is the highest intensity at which it is possible to speak comfortably	Upper limit aligns with the first ventilatory threshold (VT_1)
X	Upper limit sustainable for about 2 hours	- - -
3	Upper limit sustainable for 1 hour	Upper limit aligns with lactate threshold
Y	Upper limit sustainable for 20–30 minutes	Upper limit aligns with the second ventilatory threshold (VT_2)
4	Upper limit sustainable for 6 minutes	Upper limit aligns with VO_2max
5	Sustainable for <6 minutes	- - -

☐ LOW INTENSITY   MODERATE INTENSITY   ▨ HIGH INTENSITY

their average power by 0.95 to get an estimate of their functional threshold power (FTP). In the 80/20 Endurance intensity scale, lactate threshold pace, power, and heart rate mark the upper limit of Zone 3.

Similarly, we have noted that VO_2max intensity corresponds to the highest output an athlete can sustain for about six minutes. Thus, a six-minute time trial may serve as a suitable proxy for a proper VO_2max test. Better yet, there are known mathematical relationships between power, pace, and heart rate at VO_2max and lactate threshold. This allows athletes to use a single test to determine all of the above. In the 80/20 Endurance intensity scale, VO_2max pace, power, and heart rate mark the upper limit of Zone 4. The lower limit of Zone 4 aligns with the VT_2, which in turn aligns with critical pace and critical power. The functional correlates of this intensity, therefore, are critical pace and critical power, along with heart rate at critical pace/power.

We've noted as well that the VT_1 corresponds to the highest work rate at which an athlete can comfortably carry on a conversation. This makes the good old-fashioned "talk test" a functional correlate of the VT_1. Again, though, there are known mathematical relationships between an athlete's heart rate, pace, and power at the VT_1 and at the lactate threshold, which allows athletes to use the same test they use to determine their lactate threshold correlates to determine their VT_1 correlates as well. In the 80/20 Endurance intensity scale, VT_1 pace, power, and heart rate mark the upper limit of Zone 2.

The remaining zone boundaries have no particular functional correlates and are positioned where they are for practical reasons rather than physiological ones. For example, the lower limit of Zone 2, which is also the upper limit of Zone 1, is not associated with a specific physiological threshold. As a matter of general practice, though, efforts below this boundary are customarily reserved for warm-ups, cooldowns, and active recoveries.

In the original 80/20 Endurance zone scale (the one presented in *80/20 Running*), there were small gaps between zones 2 and 3 and between zones 3 and 4. These gaps were meant as buffers, whose function was to keep athletes from creeping out of the appropriate intensity range for specific workout types. The gap between zones 2 and 3 was considered especially important, as it is too intense for low-intensity workouts, and yet that is precisely where most recreational endurance athletes hang out in workouts intended to be done at low intensity. The gaps caused some confusion, however, so we later filled them in with Zone X, which falls between zones 2 and 3, and Zone Y, which falls between zones

3 and 4. These new lettered zones are targeted in a small number of 80/20 Endurance workouts, as there is no harm and some benefit in hitting these intensities provided it is done with intent.

If you're accustomed to using the zone calculators on the 80/20 Endurance website, you may tend to think of, say, Zone 2 swim pace as having nothing to do with Zone 2 cycling power, and Zone 5 cycling heart rate as distinct from Zone 5 run pace. But on a physiological level, each zone is basically the same in all endurance disciplines regardless of which intensity metric it's represented in. Table 2.1 summarizes the information presented in this section and shows the fundamental sameness of each individual zone, regardless of which metric is used to measure it and which sport it's applied to.

Perceived Effort

Objective metrics such as heart rate, pace, and power are not the only ways to measure intensity. It is also possible to measure intensity subjectively, as ***perceived effort***, which is an athlete's internal sense of how hard they are working. Perceived effort is in fact the most important intensity metric, for a number of reasons. First, perceived effort is the only intensity metric with no "off" switch—athletes always feel their effort during exercise. Additionally, as we will discuss in Chapter 9, perceived effort is vital to effective pacing. Moreover, perceived effort contains the most accurate and complete information about how the athlete is really doing.

For all of these reasons, endurance coaches should encourage athletes to pay attention to perceived effort in training. The most successful athletes are in tune with their bodies, able to interpret what their perceived effort is telling them, and use it to regulate their effort effectively. In these days of heavy technology dependence, athletes tend not to pay enough attention to perceived effort, which compromises the quality of their training and keeps them from finding their true limit in competition.

A high level of attunement to perceived effort helps athletes distinguish between the spirit and the letter of a workout and make appropriate adjustments that ensure they always adhere to the spirit of a workout. For example, suppose you have a cyclist perform a workout consisting of six 2-minute intervals in Zone 4. Like most workouts of this type, this one is intended to be challenging, but not overwhelming. The athlete should be able to complete the intervals within their Zone 4 power range feeling tired but able to complete at least one more interval if they had to. However, if an athlete is especially fatigued going into this workout, Zone 4 might feel harder than it normally does, and it might therefore require a high degree of effort to hit their accustomed power numbers. In these situations, athletes need to distinguish the spirit of the workout (challenging but not excruciating) from the letter of the workout (6 × 2:00 in Zone 4) and depart from the letter as much as necessary to preserve the spirit.

Being attuned to perceived effort is helpful in making such adjustments. An athlete who is attuned to their body knows what Zone 4 feels like, so when prior fatigue causes their Zone 4 power output to feel harder than normal, they can reduce their actual power as much as necessary to keep the workout from feeling harder than it should. This is one reason intensity zones encompass a range of intensities rather than just a specific point, or threshold. In most cases, adhering to the spirit of a workout on an "off" day is as simple as working at the lower end of the targeted zone rather than at the higher end.

Be sure to consistently communicate with athletes ahead of time about how the workout you prescribe is supposed to feel, and then follow up to see how it actually feels to the athlete. With those who lack body attunement, it may take a while to reach a point where they

TABLE 2.2 **HOW PERCEIVED EFFORT CORRESPONDS TO 80/20 ENDURANCE INTENSITY ZONES**

ZONE	PERCEIVED EFFORT	BENEFITS
1	1–2	Warm-ups, cooldowns, active recovery
2	3–4	Aerobic capacity, endurance, durability, tolerance
X	5	Intensive endurance
3	6	Efficiency and comfort at moderate intensity
Y	7	Typically not targeted in workouts
4	8	Aerobic capacity and fatigue resistance at faster speeds
5	9–10	Efficiency and perceived effort tolerance

☐ LOW INTENSITY　　MODERATE INTENSITY　▨ HIGH INTENSITY

are able to interpret and regulate their perceived effort well enough to consistently adhere to the spirit of workouts. Calibrating their subjective experience of various intensities against a numerical scale of perceived effort will accelerate this process. Table 2.2 shows how perceived effort ratings on a 1–10 scale correspond to the 80/20 Endurance intensity zones.

Note that the perceived effort numbers in Table 2.2 are initial ratings. A key difference between perceived effort and objective measures of exercise intensity is that perceived effort is not fixed but climbs steadily over time as fatigue accumulates. Ten minutes into a Zone 2 effort, an athlete's perceived effort rating is likely to be 3 or 4, but four hours later, that same athlete's perceived effort might be 9 or 10. In helping athletes calibrate their perceived effort, explain that each number represents how hard a given intensity feels before fatigue sets in.

Basic Endurance Workouts

Each exercise intensity contributes differently to endurance fitness. As mentioned, Zone 1 is ideal for warm-ups, cooldowns, and active recovery. Zone 2 builds aerobic capacity, endurance, durability, and overall training tolerance. Zone X develops intensive endurance, or the ability to sustain moderate efforts. Zone 3 helps athletes become more efficient and comfortable at moderate intensity, which overlaps with race pace for many endurance events. Zone Y, which is the small gap between zones 3 and 4, is generally not targeted in workouts, being a little too intense for tempo workouts (described later in this chapter) and not quite intense enough for interval workouts. Zone 4 increases aerobic capacity and fatigue resistance at faster speeds. And, finally, Zone 5 improves movement economy and pain tolerance.

Because no two zones confer the same benefits, it is necessary to regularly include workouts targeting each intensity in an athlete's training, as failure to do so will leave gaps in their fitness. Furthermore, the workouts chosen to target a given intensity need to have an appropriate duration or distance and structure. Let's consider some appropriate designs for workouts focused on low intensity (zones 1 and 2), moderate intensity (zones X and 3), and high intensity (zones 4 and 5).

Low-Intensity Workouts

There are three basic low-intensity workout types: easy workouts, recovery workouts, and long workouts. What these three workout types have in common is that they are all done entirely at low intensity. Note that easy, recovery, and long workouts are not as widely used in some endurance disciplines as they are in others. In swimming, for example, nearly every workout contains some variation in intensity. We'll address sport-specific differences in best training practices in Chapter 7.

EASY WORKOUTS

In the 80/20 system, easy workouts (also called foundation workouts) consist of a short warm-up in Zone 1 followed by a steady effort in Zone 2. In most endurance disciplines, including cycling and running, easy workouts are used more often than any other workout type because they offer the most straightforward way to maintain an 80/20 intensity balance.

As any coach or athlete familiar with the 80/20 Endurance zone scale knows, Zone 2 is a broad range. Athletes often wonder where they should be within this range. Near the upper limit to maximize the training effect? Toward the middle to minimize fatigue? The answer is whatever feels most comfortable on a given day. Perceptions aren't arbitrary; they convey information about the athlete's recovery state and readiness for training. This affords athletes the freedom to "go by feel" (within certain parameters) in easy workouts and it ensures that each of these sessions best serves the athlete's needs on that day. It is among the more common and important applications of the *principle of adaptivity*.

When an athlete feels tired from recent hard training, they are likely to be most comfortable at the lower end of Zone 2. Encouraging athletes to go extra slow on these days will prevent them from feeling compelled to maximize the benefits of their easy workouts. By holding their effort at the upper limit of Zone 2, regardless of how they feel, an athlete will needlessly exacerbate their fatigue. By the same token, when an athlete feels fresh and energetic, they're likely to be most comfortable at the top of Zone 2. If this is the case, they should go right ahead and hang out there, taking advantage of the opportunity to maximize the training effect of the workout without producing too much fatigue.

This last point deserves emphasis. To serve their intended purpose, easy workouts *must not* generate significant fatigue. Generally speaking, athletes should finish these sessions feeling better than when they started. This requires that easy workouts be reasonably short. Of course, "short" means different things for different athletes. For a novice rower, 30 minutes in Zone 2 might produce an unacceptably high level of fatigue for an easy workout, whereas an elite cyclist can ride for three hours in Zone 2 and still be only mildly fatigued (*principle of individualization*).

Easy workouts contribute to endurance fitness not so much singly as collectively. Common sense tells us that no easy workout on its own can make an athlete fitter. But a whole bunch of easy workouts will create an aggregate challenge that is indeed sufficient to stimulate large fitness gains, while leaving the athlete with plenty of residual energy to pour into harder workouts at higher intensities.

EASY WORKOUT

5:00 in Zone 1
40:00 in Zone 2

RECOVERY WORKOUTS

Recovery workouts are similar to easy workouts except that they are done at an even lower intensity (Zone 1 on the 80/20 scale). In essence, a recovery workout is an easy workout that is done soon after an especially hard workout or race, or at any other time when the athlete is highly fatigued and in need of the gentlest stimulus that qualifies as exercise. Recovery workouts should be scheduled whenever an athlete is expected to be too fatigued for an easy workout, but not so fatigued that they're better off resting. As with easy workouts, encourage athletes to self-pace their recovery workouts, choosing the effort level that feels most comfortable, all things considered.

Contrary to their name, recovery workouts do not actually facilitate recovery. Their true purpose is to administer a training stimulus that's gentle enough to *not interfere with recovery* from prior exertion. To fulfill this purpose, recovery workouts must be even shorter than easy workouts. Here again, "short" is relative. Tour de France cyclists commonly go for two-hour spins on their "rest" days without sabotaging their performance in subsequent stages. For a beginner-level runner, a more appropriate recovery session might be a 25-minute Zone 1 power walk.

RECOVERY WORKOUT

30:00 in Zone 1

LONG WORKOUTS

Like easy workouts, long workouts consist of a warm-up followed by a steady effort at low intensity. These workouts need to be long enough to produce a moderate to high level of fatigue so they can fulfill their purpose of building and maintaining endurance. The specific duration required to result in moderate to high fatigue varies widely between athletes and also within individual athletes at different times.

One long workout per week is enough to develop race-specific endurance for most athletes. Multisport athletes and ultra-endurance athletes may benefit from doing two long workouts some weeks (a long bike ride and a long run in the case of triathletes, back-to-back long runs in the case of ultrarunners). Exceeding this frequency offers little or no additional benefit and is risky, as long workouts are taxing and require significant recovery time.

Athletes who train by heart rate often find their heart rate drifting above Zone 2 toward the end of their long workouts while their power or pace remains in Zone 2. Understandably, this discrepancy between intensity metrics causes confusion for some athletes. When the athlete's heart rate monitor says they're in Zone 3 and their power meter or GPS device says they're in Zone 2, which zone are they really in? And should they slow down or hold steady?

The answer to the first of these questions is murky. It is normal for any athlete's heart rate to gradually decouple from their pace or power during long workouts. Known as *cardiac drift*, this phenomenon is caused by a loss of cardiac efficiency resulting from dehydration and a decline in mechanical efficiency resulting from fatigue. It's the second of these factors, fatigue, that makes it difficult to answer the question of which zone an athlete is really in. The truest measure of intensity is not heart rate, pace, or power but brain activity in the motor and premotor areas of the brain, where muscle work begins. In shorter workouts, brain activity is closely tied to output measures such as power and pace. As brain activity increases, power and speed increase. But in longer workouts, fatigue complicates matters. As the muscles tire, the brain has to work harder and harder to maintain any given level of power or speed, and in this sense, intensity increases despite power and speed remaining constant.

In most circumstances, heart rate is the least reliable intensity metric. This is because heart rate is affected by a lot of factors besides exercise intensity, such as caffeine intake and anxiety. However, in long workouts, heart rate gives a truer picture of intensity, rising as brain activity rises in response to muscle fatigue. The best way to handle this ambiguity as a coach is to *account* for it without being *controlled* by it. In practical terms, this means that however much time an athlete typically spends at heart rates above Zone 2 in long workouts should be anticipated in the coach's planning process. For example, if an athlete typically spends about 10 percent of their long workouts at heart rates above Zone 2, factor this into your planning to ensure their intensity balance for the week—including the next long workout—is close to 80/20. This is preferable to instructing athletes to slow down in response to a rise in heart rate during long workouts. After all, you don't want athletes to slow down in the late stages of races, so it's best not to let them get used to doing so in workouts!

The broader point to be made here is that long workouts are often challenging for athletes despite being done (mostly) at low intensity. Again, for planning purposes, all types of workouts that produce high levels of fatigue should be treated as "hard" sessions. Shorter workouts containing substantial efforts at higher intensities are not hard in the same way as long workouts done mostly at low intensity, but both result in high levels of fatigue and require more recovery time than easy workouts, so manage the frequency of these workouts with care.

Among the more important decisions to be made in planning long workouts is how long to make them in the leadup to the athlete's next important race (or "A" race). Coaches must consider both the distance of the goal event and the training history of the individual athlete in making these choices. Athletes training for shorter races don't need as much endurance as athletes training for longer races, while fitter and more experienced athletes can tolerate longer workouts than less fit and less experienced athletes. The goal in every case is to make the longest workout long enough to ensure the athlete has adequate endurance to finish strong on race day, but not so long as to create undue risk.

At extreme race distances, it is not possible for even the fittest athletes to benefit from workouts that match the goal event's duration or distance. For example, evidence suggests that any run lasting longer than five hours offers no additional endurance boost. The human body simply cannot adapt to running performed beyond this threshold. There are many running events that take more than five hours to complete, but there's no physiological rationale for running longer than five hours in training because the additional time is all risk and no reward.

There is, however, an experiential rationale for selectively exercising past the body's adaptive limit. Specifically, athletes who do this prior to participating in an ultra-endurance event have the advantage of knowing, at least to some degree, what the race is going to feel like. But because this benefit comes with risk of breakdown, athletes are best advised to reserve these extra-long efforts for other race events. For example, completing a 50-miler as a "B" race in preparation for a 100-mile "A" race is not a bad idea, as long as the two events are appropriately spaced.

LONG WORKOUT
10:00 in Zone 1
1:50:00 in Zone 2

Moderate-Intensity Workouts

The basic moderate-intensity workout types are critical power (or critical velocity) workouts, tempo workouts, steady state workouts, and fast finish workouts. All are effective tools for increasing the speed that athletes are able to sustain for moderate durations and increasing the duration that athletes can sustain moderate speeds. To fulfill their purpose, moderate-intensity workouts must be hard enough to challenge the athlete's current limits but not so hard that they go beyond the athlete's adaptive limit.

To help you keep your athletes within this range, we present two examples of each moderate-intensity workout type (excluding fast finish workouts). The first example is a lighter version that represents a good starting point for athletes at lower levels of fitness. The second is a "maximal" version that should be given only to experienced athletes who are close to peak fitness.

CRITICAL POWER/CRITICAL VELOCITY WORKOUTS

Critical power/critical velocity (CP/CV) workouts target the second ventilatory threshold (VT$_2$), which falls at the bottom end of Zone 4 in the 80/20 Endurance intensity scale. You will recall that this intensity is sustainable for 20 to 30 minutes in race conditions. CP/CV workouts thus take the form of long intervals separated by recovery periods, as this structure enables the athlete to complete a relatively high volume of work at this intensity without overexerting themselves. Straddling the boundary between moderate and high intensity, CP/CV workouts provide a great return on investment, as athletes can handle more work at the VT_2 than they can at higher intensities, yet the sessions are intense enough to confer benefits that gentler moderate-intensity workouts miss.

CRITICAL POWER/
CRITICAL VELOCITY WORKOUT

5:00 in Zone 1

5:00 in Zone 2

4 × (4:00 at CV or CP/2:00 in Zone 1)

5:00 in Zone 1

5:00 in Zone 2

MAXIMAL CRITICAL POWER/
CRITICAL VELOCITY WORKOUT

5:00 in Zone 1

15:00 in Zone 2

8 × (4:00 at CV or CP/2:00 in Zone 1)

5:00 in Zone 1

15:00 in Zone 2

TEMPO WORKOUTS

Also called threshold workouts, ***tempo workouts*** consist of one or more extended segments performed at or near lactate threshold intensity, which aligns with the upper limit of Zone 3. Because the body is able to sustain a relatively stable metabolic state at lactate threshold intensity, dividing these workouts into multiple intervals separated by recovery periods does not greatly increase the amount of work that can be done without overtaxing the athlete. One or two Zone 3 efforts with a combined duration of less than 60 minutes will do the job.

TEMPO WORKOUT

5:00 in Zone 1

10:00 in Zone 2

2 × 10:00 in Zone 3/5:00 in Zone 1

5:00 in Zone 1

10:00 in Zone 2

MAXIMAL TEMPO WORKOUT

5:00 in Zone 1

10:00 in Zone 2

2 × 24:00 in Zone 3/5:00 in Zone 1

5:00 in Zone 1

10:00 in Zone 2

STEADY STATE WORKOUTS

Steady state workouts are the least intense workouts targeting moderate intensity, typically comprising a single, prolonged effort in Zone X. In prescribing steady state workouts, aim to make the Zone X segment long enough to result in a moderate to moderately high level of fatigue. Naturally, the length of the Zone X interval will increase along with the athlete's fitness (*principle of progression*).

STEADY STATE WORKOUT	MAXIMAL STEADY STATE WORKOUT
5:00 in Zone 1	**5:00 in Zone 1**
10:00 in Zone 2	**10:00 in Zone 2**
25:00 in Zone X	**1:20:00 in Zone X**
5:00 in Zone 1	**5:00 in Zone 1**
10:00 in Zone 2	**10:00 in Zone 2**

FAST FINISH WORKOUTS

Fast finish workouts are essentially easy workouts that end with a short segment at moderate intensity. They allow coaches to administer small doses of moderate intensity as appropriate, particularly during off-season training (the period between race-focused macrocycles) and base training (the early part of a macrocycle), as well as in recovery weeks. There is no maximal fast finish workout offered because these workouts are not intended to be especially challenging.

FAST FINISH WORKOUT

5:00 in Zone 1
45:00 in Zone 2
10:00 in Zone 3

High-Intensity Workouts

The key difference between high intensity and both low and moderate intensity is that small amounts of high-intensity training produce significant fitness benefits. This gives endurance coaches latitude to implement high-intensity training in a number of ways. In addition to challenging interval sessions targeting zones 4 and 5, which serve to maximize aerobic capacity, fatigue resistance at faster speeds, movement economy, and pain tolerance, lighter workouts featuring modest doses of high-intensity work can be put to a variety of uses.

Specifically, these lighter workouts fit well in the off-season, where they function as an efficient way to maintain an adequate fitness baseline, as well as in base training, when an athlete is not yet close to peak fitness, and in recovery weeks, where regeneration is the priority. These same workouts are also appropriate as a secondary training stimulus when athletes are more focused on developing fitness at moderate intensity and their most challenging workouts are in the form of CP/CV intervals, tempos, and steady states.

The basic high-intensity workout types are speed intervals, lactate intervals, hill repetitions, and fartlek workouts. As in the previous section, we will present two examples of each workout type: a lighter version that represents a good starting point for athletes at lower levels of fitness and a "maximal" version that should be given only to experienced athletes who are close to peak fitness.

SPEED INTERVALS WORKOUTS

Speed intervals are, as their name indicates, performed at very high intensity (Zone 5) and are necessarily very short. Generally speaking, the duration of the intervals determines their specific intensity, with shorter intervals being completed at faster speeds than longer ones. For example, 20-second intervals would likely be done as sprints, while 90-second intervals would be performed toward the low end of Zone 5. In speed workouts that are intended to be highly challenging, athletes should be encouraged to approach the entire interval set as a 9-out-of-10 effort, finishing the session with one or two repetitions left in the tank.

SPEED INTERVALS WORKOUT	MAXIMAL SPEED INTERVALS WORKOUT
5:00 in Zone 1	5:00 in Zone 1
10:00 in Zone 2	10:00 in Zone 2
6 × (0:30 in Zone 5/1:30 in Zone 1)	20 × (1:00 in Zone 5/2:00 in Zone 1)
5:00 in Zone 1	5:00 in Zone 1
10:00 in Zone 2	10:00 in Zone 2

LACTATE INTERVALS WORKOUTS

Lactate intervals is an umbrella term for intervals performed at or near functional VO_2max, or the highest velocity or power that can be sustained for about 6 minutes, which aligns with the upper limit of Zone 4. Unlike speed intervals, which have to be short because the required intensity cannot be sustained for an extended period, lactate intervals can vary in length. An example of a short interval is 30 × 30 seconds in Zone 4 with 15 seconds of recovery in Zone 1 after each interval and a 3-minute Zone 2 "set break" after every tenth interval. In this type of format, extremely short active recoveries make the workout quite challenging despite the brevity of the Zone 4 repetitions. Examples of longer lactate intervals workouts are given below.

LACTATE INTERVALS WORKOUT

5:00 in Zone 1
10:00 in Zone 2
4 × (2:00 in Zone 4/2:00 in Zone 1)
5:00 in Zone 1
10:00 in Zone 2

MAXIMAL LACTATE INTERVALS WORKOUT

5:00 in Zone 1
10:00 in Zone 2
8 × (2:00 in Zone 4/2:00 in Zone 1)
5:00 in Zone 1
10:00 in Zone 2

HILL REPETITIONS WORKOUTS

Hill repetitions are identical to speed intervals and lactate intervals except that the intervals are performed on an incline. This type of workout applies to certain endurance disciplines—e.g., running, road cycling, mountain biking, skimo. In these sports, hill repetitions provide specific preparation for climbing in competition and they also add a strength- and power-building dimension to high-intensity training.

HILL REPETITIONS WORKOUT

5:00 in Zone 1
10:00 in Zone 2
6 × (0:30 uphill in Zone 5/1:30 in Zone 1)
5:00 in Zone 1
10:00 in Zone 2

MAXIMAL HILL REPETITIONS WORKOUT

5:00 in Zone 1
10:00 in Zone 2
16 × (1:00 uphill in Zone 5/2:00 in Zone 1)
5:00 in Zone 1
10:00 in Zone 2

FARTLEK WORKOUTS

Fartlek workouts are a lighter form of high-intensity workout. Slightly less structured than speed intervals and lactate intervals, they can be thought of as easy workouts with a few short surges in zones 4 or 5. Although the term "fartlek" is specific to running, this type of workout is useful in most endurance disciplines. Whereas harder high-intensity workout types serve to maximize certain aspects of endurance fitness, such as aerobic capacity, fartlek workouts are intended to start the process of developing these fitness aspects or to maintain them once they've been fully developed. They're especially useful during offseason and base training, as well as in recovery weeks. No maximal fartlek workout is given because these workouts are not meant to be especially challenging.

FARTLEK WORKOUT

5:00 in Zone 1

10:00 in Zone 2

8 × (1:00 in Zone 4/2:00 in Zone 1)

5:00 in Zone 1

10:00 in Zone 2

Race-Pace Workouts

Athletes tend to perform better in races when they've had practice at their anticipated race intensity (*principle of specificity*), which is why workouts targeting the specific pace or power output associated with this intensity are essential. The benefits of these sessions include increased comfort and efficiency at race intensity and improved pacing ability. They're also helpful in setting race performance goals.

Unlike the other workout types discussed in this chapter, race-pace workouts target specific power or pace numbers rather than zones, which are far too broad to be useful in these cases. For example, half-marathon pace for a runner with a personal-best time of 1:43:00 is 4:53 per kilometer. The Zone 3 pace range for a runner of this ability is 4:42 to 5:03 per km. Hence, technically, the runner's half-marathon pace falls within Zone 3, but a workout intended to give this runner practice at race pace should target the exact pace of 4:53 per km rather than Zone 3, as it's not really a half-marathon pace workout otherwise.

RACE-PACE WORKOUT

1 km in Zone 1

1 km in Zone 2

3 × 5 km at half-marathon race pace/1:00 rest

1 km in Zone 1

1 km in Zone 2

FROM BUILDING BLOCKS TO BUILDING

There's a big difference between a pile of bricks and a brick house. Similarly, there's a big difference between a collection of workouts and an effective training program. Having identified the fundamental building blocks of endurance training and the intensities they target, we will now turn our attention to intensity balance. This is where coaches can deliver real value to their athletes, combining the various workout types in a way that maximizes their effectiveness.

Guidelines for Balancing Training Intensities

KEY POINTS

⟋ The 80/20 rule of intensity balance should be interpreted as a flexible guideline rather than as a rigid law.

⟋ To get the intensity balance right for each individual athlete, consider the type of athlete, the type of race they are training for, and where they are in the training process.

⟋ The optimal balance of low, moderate, and high intensities varies between individual athletes. Because most athletes can attain peak performance at more than one intensity ratio, "optimal" is a range, not a precise point.

The world's best endurance athletes do not perform exactly 80 percent of their training at low intensity and 20 percent at moderate to high intensity. Nevertheless, the 80/20 rule serves as a useful starting point for discussing how endurance coaches should manage intensity balance in their athletes' training. By qualifying this rule with the necessary exceptions and caveats rooted in best practice and the core principles introduced in Chapter 1, we can establish a flexible set of guidelines for endurance coaches to apply.

There is no magic in round numbers.

More than 100 separate studies have looked at training intensity distribution in elite endurance athletes. In none of these studies have athletes been found to do exactly 80 percent of their training at low intensity and precisely 20 percent at moderate to high intensity. The ratio is always close to 80/20, but never a perfect bull's-eye. This suggests that precision is not important in the effort to balance training intensities for maximum fitness.

An analogy will help us see why. To maintain a stable body weight, it's necessary to consume a certain average number of food calories daily. But does a person have to consume exactly this number of calories every day? No. The reason is that calories aren't numbers—they are physical things that interact with the body in complex ways. A person who eats a little more than normal in a given meal is likely to feel more energetic afterward, and, as a result, they will be more active and burn more calories. They are also likely to feel more full and consequently eat less in their next meal, negating the potential weight-increasing effect of the extra calories. Likewise, if the person eats less than normal in a given meal, the opposite will happen, to the same effect. This is how people maintain a stable body weight despite seldom, if ever, eating the precise number of daily calories required to keep from gaining or losing weight.

Something similar occurs in endurance training. An athlete who aims for an 80/20 intensity balance, but never hits it perfectly, is likely to get the same desired result as an athlete who somehow manages to nail the precise ratio. Like calories, workouts done at various intensities are not merely data but physical realities that interact with athletes' bodies in complex ways. To give a basic example, an athlete who exercises a bit more intensely than normal during a given period is likely to feel more fatigued afterward, causing the athlete to exercise a bit less intensely than normal during the next period, such that over time everything balances out.

What's more, even if an athlete tried to do exactly 80 percent of their training at low intensity and precisely 20 percent at moderate to high intensity, they would fall short of perfection. In controlled studies where researchers have tried to get athletes to maintain a perfect 80/20 intensity balance, the athletes invariably missed the target, which was okay because they improved significantly as a result of getting close to the 80/20 split. The take-home lesson is that any good-faith effort to adhere to an 80/20 intensity balance will yield equal fitness, regardless of the exact ratio achieved.

Intensity balance varies depending on how intensity is measured.

There are four main ways to measure intensity in endurance training: pace (or speed), power, heart rate, and perceived effort. Studies have found that each of these metrics yields a different intensity balance when applied to the same period of training. Specifically, when heart rate is used to measure intensity, athletes are found to spend more time at moderate to high intensity. The reason is that, once elevated, heart rate takes time to come back down, whereas changes in pace and power are registered instantaneously. And when intensity is measured through perceived effort ratings, athletes are found to spend even more time at high intensity than when heart rate is used. That's because athletes tend to rate their effort for the entire workout, not individual segments, so a 45-minute interval workout is rated as 45 minutes at high intensity even though it is only the work intervals that are done at high intensity. To be clear, the training itself is the same regardless of how intensity is measured—only the measurements differ.

Such discrepancies can be mitigated to some degree by fudging the math in interval-type workouts. Specifically, we recommend that each interval set be counted entirely as time spent at high intensity. For example, an interval set comprising 5 × 3:00 in Zone 4/2:00 in Zone 1 should be counted as 25 minutes at high intensity even though the Zone 1 recoveries are done at low intensity. The rationale for this practice is that counting the entire interval block as time spent at high intensity more accurately reflects the physiological stressfulness of the interval set. Heart rate monitoring would show this, as it's very unlikely that an athlete's heart rate will drop all the way down to Zone 1 in the 2 minutes between Zone 4 efforts. Pace or power monitoring, however, would not reflect this reality. The exceptions are interval sets with recoveries lasting longer than 2 minutes, which do allow enough time for the heart rate to settle down and aren't as stressful to the body.

Even with this bit of fudging, discrepancies will remain between intensity balances calculated with different metrics. For coaches, the measurement-dependent nature of intensity is one more reminder that it is not possible to regulate intensity balance with exactitude. It's a fool's errand to strive for unattainable perfection in this area.

Another practical implication of the irreconcilability of the various intensity metrics relates to planning. For consistency's sake, it's best to select one metric to calculate intensity balance in the process of planning an athlete's training. Athletes can still utilize different metrics to monitor and regulate intensity as they execute the workouts, but the coach is better off not mixing and matching metrics when creating a plan.

The 80/20 rule of intensity balance does not apply to every workout.

One way for an athlete to adhere to an approximate 80/20 intensity balance in training is to complete 8 out of every 10 minutes of every workout at low intensity and the remaining 2 minutes at moderate to high intensity. A cyclist, for example, might ride for 48 minutes in Zone 2 and 12 minutes in Zone 3 on Monday, ride for 32 minutes in Zone 2 and 8 minutes in Zone 5 on Tuesday, ride for 80 minutes in Zone 2 and 20 minutes in Zone X on Wednesday, and so on. Although this approach does conform to the 80/20 rule of intensity balance, it is not an effective way to train. Once again, we know this because elite athletes don't train this way. However, a majority of recreational endurance athletes do train this way, albeit unwittingly.

Numerous studies have found that recreational endurance athletes spend a lot of time at moderate intensity in almost every workout. And we know from other research that these athletes get fitter and perform better when they adopt the elite approach of doing most of their workouts entirely at low intensity and a few workouts mostly at higher intensities. If you were to randomly select a week of training from an elite athlete's schedule, you would probably find something very close to an 80/20 intensity balance, yet it's unlikely that any single workout within the week would be close to 80/20. Table 3.1 offers an illustration of how you might balance intensities on a weekly timescale. Note that while an elite endurance athlete would likely train at a much higher volume, the general approach would be the same.

TABLE 3.1 **STANDARD TRAINING WEEK**

	TRAINING	INTENSITY BALANCE
Monday	Rest	---
Tuesday	38:00 in Zones 1–2 22:00 in Zone 3	63/37
Wednesday	48:00 in Zones 1–2	100/0
Thursday	48:00 in Zones 1–2	100/0
Friday	34:00 in Zones 1–2 10:00 in Zone 4 6:00 in Zone 5	68/32
Saturday	48:00 in Zones 1–2	100/0
Sunday	1:00:00 in Zones 1–2 30:00 in Zone X	67/33
TOTAL	**4:36:00 in Zones 1–2** **1:08:00 in Zones X–5**	**80/20**

In planning your athletes' training, focus on maintaining an appropriate intensity balance at the weekly timescale and beyond rather than from day to day.

Regulate intensity balance on a time or session basis.

Observational studies have shown that elite cyclists, runners, swimmers, and triathletes all spend close to 80 percent of their *total training time* at low intensity and the rest at moderate to high intensity. Elite cross-country skiers and rowers, meanwhile, do about 80 percent (or eight in ten) of their *training sessions* entirely at low intensity and devote the remaining 20 percent (or two in ten) to moderate-intensity and high-intensity efforts. But because their harder workouts aren't done entirely at higher intensities, these athletes end up spending close to 90 percent of their total training time at low intensity. This demonstrates that the 80/20 rule of intensity balance applies differently in different sports, with elite endurance athletes in some sports applying the rule on a time basis, and others applying it on a session basis.

The 80/20 Endurance training methodology is all about emulating the best practices of elite athletes. So if you coach cross-country skiers or rowers, balance their training intensities in the same way as elite athletes in these sports, devoting two out of every ten training sessions to higher intensities, which will result in about 90 percent of total training time at low intensity. And if you coach cyclists, runners, swimmers, or triathletes, balance their training intensities the same way as elite athletes in these sports, ensuring that they spend about 80 percent of their total training time at low intensity, which can be achieved by devoting roughly one in three workouts to higher intensities.

Athletes in some endurance sports, including running and swimming, typically measure training volume in distance rather than time. While it is feasible to measure intensity balance in terms of distance, it is somewhat impractical because the relationship between time and distance is not linear—athletes cover more distance in equal time at higher intensities. An athlete who spends 80 percent of their training time at low intensity generally ends up doing about 75 percent of their total distance at low intensity.

Don't try to maintain a consistent intensity balance at all times.

Maintaining an approximate 80/20 intensity balance is necessary to maximize endurance fitness. Thus, whenever an athlete is actively pursuing maximal fitness, their training should adhere to an 80/20 intensity split. When athletes aren't pursuing maximal endurance fitness, they need not obey the 80/20 rule.

During the off-season, for example, when there are no imminent races and the athlete is training at a maintenance level, keeping an 80/20 intensity balance is okay, but it's seldom done at the elite level. Instead, these athletes do something closer to 90/10 during the off-season, with just a sprinkling of work at higher intensities—enough to maintain a higher baseline of fitness than they would get from doing all of their training at low intensity, but not so much as to interfere with the regenerative purpose of the off-season (*principle of purpose*). Table 3.2 provides an example of a week of off-season training. As in the previous example, an elite endurance athlete would likely train at a higher volume, even in the off-season, but the approach would be the same.

Another period in which the 80/20 rule of intensity balance doesn't apply is when the athlete's top priority is improving body composition rather than building fitness for racing performance. Research has shown that the most effective training program for fat loss is one

TABLE 3.2 **STANDARD OFF-SEASON TRAINING WEEK**

	TRAINING	LOW INTENSITY	MODERATE/ HIGH INTENSITY
Monday	Rest	---	---
Tuesday	**FARTLEK WORKOUT** 5:00 in Zone 1 10:00 in Zone 2 10 × 0:20 in Zone 5/1:40 in Zone 1 15:00 in Zone 2	30:00	20:00
Wednesday	**EASY WORKOUT** 5:00 in Zone 1 40:00 in Zone 2	45:00	---
Thursday	**EASY WORKOUT** 5:00 in Zone 1 40:00 in Zone 2	45:00	---
Friday	**FAST FINISH WORKOUT** 5:00 in Zone 1 30:00 in Zone 2 10:00 in Zone 3	35:00	10:00
Saturday	**EASY WORKOUT** 5:00 in Zone 1 40:00 in Zone 2	45:00	---
Sunday	**ENDURANCE WORKOUT** 5:00 in Zone 1 1:25:00 in Zone 2	1:30:00	---
TOTAL		**4:50:00 (90%)**	**30:00 (10%)**

*Recall that in interval-type workouts, the entire interval block counts as time spent at moderate/high intensity provided the recovery periods between intervals are no more than 2 minutes long.

in which high-intensity predominates, which, of course, is precisely the opposite of the best way to train for endurance fitness. Recreational endurance athletes often make the mistake of trying to pursue race fitness and weight loss simultaneously, but these goals aren't compatible. If you find yourself coaching an athlete who wants to shed excess body fat, set aside a few weeks to focus on this goal with appropriate methods before shifting to race-focused fitness building and 80/20 training. The Racing Weight plans available at 8020endurance.com show how triathletes and runners can adapt their training to optimize body composition.

Race distance dictates a different balance of moderate and high intensity.

You will have noticed that moderate intensity and high intensity are lumped together in the 80/20 intensity ratio. The reason is that there is no fixed rule governing how moderate intensity and high intensity should be balanced within the 20 percent bucket. The optimal balance of moderate- and high-intensity training varies depending on the type of race the athlete is preparing for and where they are in the training process.

The dividing line between moderate and high intensity falls at critical power/velocity, which equates to an effort that is sustainable for 20 to 30 minutes. This means that races (or race segments in the case of triathlon and other multisport events) requiring less than 20 to 30 minutes to complete are performed at high intensity, while most longer races are performed at moderate intensity. The *principle of specificity* dictates that athletes should spend some time training at or near the intensity of their upcoming race, which means athletes preparing for races lasting less than 20 to 30 minutes should spend more time training at high intensity than athletes preparing for longer races, who in turn should spend more time training at moderate intensity. Both groups should limit their combined work at moderate and high intensity to about 20 percent of total training volume. But within this 20 percent, the balance between moderate and high intensity will differ according to race specialization.

Remember that the principle of specificity extends only so far, however. Athletes preparing for shorter races should still do some training at moderate intensity even though they compete at a higher intensity, and athletes preparing for longer races should sometimes train at high intensity even though they compete at a lower intensity. In fact, the only period in which athletes really need to prioritize the intensity at which they compete is the specific phase of training encompassing the last several weeks before competition. Prior to this period, it is helpful for athletes to build fitness at other intensities, thereby creating a better foundation upon which to layer race-specific fitness. We will discuss how priorities for the athlete evolve over the course of a training cycle in Chapter 5.

Optimal intensity balance may vary for individual athletes and even change over time.

It's important to recognize that studies on training intensity balance report average results rather than individual results. Controlled studies involving recreational endurance athletes have found that, at a group level, an 80/20 intensity balance maximizes improvement, but within a given group, some individuals benefit more than others. Similarly, observational studies involving elite endurance athletes have found that most of them come close to an 80/20 intensity balance, but some elites spend a little more time at low intensity and others a little less.

None of this should surprise us. Each athlete is physiologically unique—the *principle of individualization* is grounded in this fundamental truth. Hence, while all athletes respond similarly to various training stimuli, the finer details define an individual athlete's optimal training formula. Still, you will not find an athlete who responds better to a 100/0 or 20/80 intensity balance than they do to an 80/20 balance. With respect to intensity balance, applying the principle of individualization is a three-step process.

Step 1: Use the standard 80/20 intensity balance as a starting point for each athlete. You have to start somewhere, after all, and even if it turns out that an 80/20 split is not optimal for a given athlete, it won't be far off the mark, and as such it is certain to yield good results as you work your way through steps two and three.

Step 2: Pay close attention to how the athlete responds to various training stimuli. In particular, pay attention to whether the athlete has a weak or strong response to low-intensity, moderate-intensity, and high-intensity training, and whether they have a low or high tolerance for each level of intensity. An athlete who has a strong response to a particular intensity gains fitness quickly when exposed to it, whereas an athlete who has a weak response gains fitness slowly. Likewise, an athlete who has a high tolerance for a certain intensity can do a lot of it without entering into a state of nonfunctional overreaching, whereas an athlete who has a low tolerance can't.

The statistician knows that this effort to classify athletes by their responsiveness to, and tolerance for, different intensities results in 64 distinct intensity profiles (i.e., $(2^2)^3$). A given athlete might, for example, respond to low intensity strongly and tolerate it well, respond to moderate intensity weakly but tolerate it well, and respond to high intensity well but tolerate it poorly. In reality, the number of athlete types is much greater than 64 because athletes differ in their responses and tolerances to various intensities by degrees rather than in the binary fashion implied by the example offered. In any case, the coach must pay attention to learn how each athlete responds to and tolerates different intensities.

Step 3: Adjust the athlete's intensity balance based on what you learn about them (*principle of adaptivity*). Generally speaking, a high tolerance for a specific intensity is a green light to do more of it, while a low tolerance signals the opposite. A weak response to a specific intensity tells you that you may need to give a little extra attention to that intensity. On the other hand, a strong response indicates that you can afford to use a lighter touch with a given intensity, timing and apportioning its usage to gain desired results with minimal risk. If you observe that an athlete has a strong response to high intensity but a low tolerance for it, you might sprinkle this intensity very lightly into the athlete's training, or else focus on it only in the final weeks before competition.

Note that each athlete's intensity profile is likely to evolve over time. Research suggests that novice athletes have a lower tolerance for high-intensity training than experienced athletes, while responsiveness to moderate-intensity training tends to decrease as fitness increases. Both tolerance for and responsiveness to training at all intensities tend to decline with age. Although this decline typically begins in an athlete's thirties, it is very gradual at first and accelerates in succeeding decades. These patterns aren't universal, however, so you can't just assume that a beginner athlete will have a low tolerance for high intensity, or that an experienced athlete will lose responsiveness to moderate intensity, or that an athlete in their forties will have a lower tolerance for and responsiveness to all intensities than they did in their twenties. Hence, the job of paying attention to how athletes respond to training and adapting accordingly is never done. You must always remain open to adjusting an athlete's personal intensity formula.

Throughout the process of individualizing intensity balance, bear in mind that your main goal is to prepare athletes for the specific demands of racing, not to play to their strengths or work around their weaknesses. Suppose you have an athlete with a high tolerance for high intensity and a low tolerance for low intensity. Despite this makeup, the athlete competes in ultramarathons, which are contested at low to moderate intensity. Playing to this athlete's strengths by having them do a lot more work at high intensity than the typical elite ultrarunner will not prepare them for maximum success in competition. Regardless of the athlete's intensity profile, the intensity distribution of their training needs to be reasonably close to the norm for their primary event, hence close to 80/20.

Optimal intensity balance is a range, not a point.

The preceding section might have given you the impression that, although the optimal intensity balance varies somewhat between individual athletes and also within individuals over time, an exact optimal intensity balance does exist for each athlete at any given time. In fact, this is not the case. Evidence from the lab and the field suggest that any given athlete can attain maximal fitness at any point within a narrow range of intensity ratios.

Here's why: The primary determinant of fitness is training load, which factors together both the intensity and the volume of training. Studies have shown that when the training load is held constant, athletes improve by equal amounts on somewhat different intensity ratios provided that the majority of their training time is spent at low intensity. Likewise, it has often been observed that when elite athletes change teams or coaches, which involves some shifting of intensities, their subsequent competitive performances tend to align with past standards. What both types of evidence reveal is that different combinations of volume and intensity can result in a training load that maximizes a given athlete's fitness. To be clear, these combinations lie within a narrow range, and while they are never far from 80/20 on the intensity side, it would be inaccurate to imply that a single, perfect formula exists for any athlete. This point is a fitting one to conclude with, as training load management is the subject of the next chapter.

Guidelines for Measuring and Manipulating Training Loads

KEY POINTS

⫽ Training load, which factors in both the volume and the intensity of training, is the primary determinant of fitness. Except in cases where an athlete is currently overtraining, it is almost impossible to increase fitness except by increasing the training load.

⫽ Each athlete has a training load "sweet spot"—the highest training load that the athlete's body can beneficially adapt to. This level of training is not indefinitely sustainable; hence, it should be built up to gradually and imposed on the athlete for brief periods only before an important race.

⫽ Throughout the training process, coaches should pay attention to quantitative and subjective measures of load and use the information to ensure the athlete is not training too hard or too easy at any point.

Endurance training is appealingly straightforward. The process can almost be reduced to a formula, with inputs on one side and outputs on the other. At the most basic level, there is only one input (training load) and one output (fitness). The relationship between training load and fitness is so direct and uncomplicated, in fact, that training load is often used as a measure of fitness by scientists and mathematically inclined coaches. How fit is the athlete? As fit as the training they've done.

Up to a point, we hasten to add. Athletes can't just keep getting fitter and fitter by training more and more. There's a limit to how fit a human being can get, a limit that is determined by the body's capacity to absorb and adapt to training. The ultimate goal of endurance training, then, is to find this limit, or training load *sweet spot*.

The sweet spot is different for each athlete. Elite endurance athletes, obviously, are able to absorb and adapt to higher training loads, which results in higher levels of fitness. Although athletes with less-favorable genetics cannot get quite as fit as the elites, they can discover their own training load sweet spot by using the same training methods.

The hallmark characteristics of elite endurance training are high volume and an 80/20 intensity balance. Why these and not some other combination of training characteristics? Because no other combination allows athletes to attain their true training load sweet spot. A closer look at the mathematics of training load makes this point clear. In Chapter 1, we introduced the concept of *chronic training load* (CTL), which is calculated as an exponentially weighted average of an athlete's training load over the past several weeks. It has been shown that elite athletes in various endurance sports maintain CTLs of 150 to 160 during peak training periods. This range therefore represents the training load sweet spot for elite endurance athletes. And the reason these athletes train the way they do is that a CTL of 150 or higher is not achievable any other way.

Let's first consider what would happen if an athlete tried to attain an equal or greater level of fitness by doing a higher percentage of their training at high intensity. This isn't a crazy idea, for as we know, high intensity makes a far bigger contribution than low intensity to CTL per unit of time. But this contribution comes at a cost, and that is fatigue. While a little high-intensity training goes a long way, more than a little results in overreaching, even among those with favorable genetics. An elite athlete who trained mostly at high intensity would never be able to tolerate a sufficient amount to reach a CTL of 150 to 160. For example, a runner seeking to hit the 150 mark with a training program consisting entirely of high-intensity workouts would somehow have to run in Zone 5 for 72 minutes a day for 42 straight days.

Now let's consider what would happen if an athlete tried to attain an equal or greater level of fitness by going in the other direction, doing not 80 percent but 100 percent of their training at low intensity. The problem here is that small amounts of low intensity, unlike high intensity, make a small contribution to CTL. Hence, an athlete who trained entirely at low intensity would have to maintain an astronomical volume—specifically, three hours of Zone 2 running every day for six weeks—to breach the 150 CTL threshold.

An 80/20 intensity balance, however, allows athletes to have it both ways, combining low-intensity training and moderate- to high-intensity training in proportions that enable them to attain the highest training load possible without overreaching (*principle of balance*). Granted, most endurance athletes cannot reach a CTL of 150 or higher by any means, but an 80/20 intensity balance ensures that even the least genetically favored athletes will discover their personal training load sweet spot, whatever it may be. Regardless of age, ability, or experience, the surest way for an athlete to realize their full fitness potential is to build up to the highest volume of training at an 80/20 intensity ratio that yields positive returns for them.

There is, of course, much more to be said on the subject of managing training loads than the advice to train at a high volume and maintain an 80/20 intensity balance. The balance of this chapter provides additional guidelines for measuring and controlling training loads with the athletes you coach.

Establish an appropriate starting point.

The first week of a new macrocycle is an important one. It's an opportunity to get athletes started on the right foot with their training load progression. The training load in this week should be big enough to begin the process of making the athlete fitter but not so big that it overwhelms them. To strike this balance, the training you prescribe for this week will need to be slightly greater than the athlete's recent training. If you've been working with the athlete for some time, you will have this information already. For a new client, you'll want to gather it before you begin planning.

It's helpful to know not just the athlete's recent training history but also their extended history. To see why, let's consider two athletes, Sam and Jan. They each trained 6 hours last week and both of them are ready to start a fresh macrocycle under your guidance. If this were all the information you had about Sam and Jan, you might decide to increase the training load of both athletes equally over the first few weeks. But what if Sam has successfully trained 11 hours per week in the past, whereas Jan has never trained more than 6 hours per week and is recovering from an injury? Given this additional information, you will probably want to plan differently for the two athletes, taking advantage of Sam's proven tolerance for higher training loads by increasing the load more aggressively, while taking a more cautious approach with Jan (*principle of individualization*).

While not the most realistic example, it makes the point. The initial training load that is most appropriate will differ between athletes depending on both their recent and their extended training history. In all cases, though, the goal is to prescribe training that stimulates fitness gains in a way that is manageable for the individual athlete.

Don't predetermine the endpoint.

An athlete's training load should increase gradually throughout the macrocycle (except in recovery weeks), peaking one to four weeks before their most important "A" race. That peak training week is even more important than the first week of the cycle, as it will determine how much fitness the athlete will carry into the race. It's tempting to plan this week well ahead of time, perhaps even at the very beginning of the macrocycle, so you know how much fitness the athlete will have come race day. Unfortunately, that's not how it works.

Planning a week of peak training months in advance is like forecasting the weather months in advance. You can do it in a general way, but not with precision. The *principle of adaptivity* reminds endurance coaches to plan in pencil, respecting the inherent unpredictability of training outcomes. Coaches have no guarantee that a peak training week planned at the beginning of a macrocycle will be appropriate for the athlete when they get there. It might be too heavy or too light or contain individual workouts that are too hard or too easy. The process leading up to that point will decide which of these possibilities is true.

It would be an overstatement to say that a coach has no clue what sort of peak training load will be appropriate for an athlete when mapping a season. With knowledge of an athlete's extended training history a coach can anticipate, with some degree of accuracy, where their athlete will end up in the current training cycle. Specifically, the athlete's training load sweet spot is likely to be close to where it's been in the past. But there are plenty of exceptions. If you're working with a beginner, they won't have a prior sweet spot to go by. If you're working with an athlete who's training for a different race distance than they have in the past, their extended training history will be of limited value. And if an athlete you're working with experiences an unexpected setback during the training cycle, chances are they won't be able to match their past peak training loads.

Further complicating matters is the fact that an athlete's sweet spot changes over time. Each completed macrocycle increases the athlete's training tolerance, lifting their training load sweet spot step by step until they reach their ultimate sweet spot—the highest training load their body will ever be able to absorb and adapt to. This process can take many years to reach completion.

Aging, of course, has the opposite effect. Beyond a certain age—which varies between individuals based on a variety of factors, including genetics and injury history—training tolerance begins to decrease gradually. For all of these reasons, it's best to plan peak training loads in pencil, if at all. Focus instead on the process of building the training load step by step from the first week of the macrocycle to the peak week.

There are some circumstances in which coaches need to make definite assumptions about where an athlete will end up with their training load in a given macrocycle. The obvious examples are ready-made training plans designed for general use by multiple athletes and custom training plans designed for use by individual athletes who will not be actively monitored throughout the macrocycle. In these cases, it's best to plan a somewhat conservative load progression that should be close to optimal for the athlete, even allowing for a few minor setbacks. Deliver the plan with instructions for the athlete to listen to their body and adjust workouts appropriately as they go.

Consider time available and rate of load increase.

In addition to the individual athlete's training load sweet spot, two other factors to consider in manipulating training loads are *time available* and *rate of load increase*. Time available refers to the amount of time between the start and the endpoint of a training cycle. More time obviously allows for greater increases in load—an athlete can get a lot fitter in twenty weeks than they can in ten weeks. The rate of load increase is just that—how quickly the training load rises over time—and is commonly measured as the ratio of acute training load to chronic training load.

Time available and rate of load increase are interdependent, which is why we're discussing them together. It's generally preferable to allow enough time between the start of a training cycle and the next "A" race so that the training load can be increased at a conservative rate, as this minimizes the risk of nonfunctional overreaching. When the time available is less than ideal, the training load will need to be increased at a more aggressive rate to yield peak fitness and the associated risk must be accepted.

Allowing more time than necessary to attain peak fitness carries risks of its own. While it might seem harmless, extra time means extra opportunities for things to go wrong, and it can be difficult for both the athlete and the coach to stay focused on a single training mission for months on end. Things usually work out best when there is a slight sense of urgency throughout the process.

The 24-week rule is a good guideline for macrocycle duration. This rule states that a macrocycle should not exceed 24 weeks in length, and it exists for the simple reason that it is difficult to find an example of an athlete who succeeded in building fitness for longer than 24 weeks in pursuit of peak race performance (*principle of cyclicality*). It's acceptable, and sometimes necessary, to schedule races further than 24 weeks out from the starting point of an athletic "season," but the training for a season lasting longer than 24 weeks should not be planned with the expectation that the athlete will continually build fitness the entire time. In these cases, the season should be divided into two or more cycles linked by brief regenerative periods in which the training load is reduced and the athlete voluntarily gives up a bit of fitness to avoid overreaching.

Athletes training for multi-hour events, who are currently at a modest level of fitness, will need a full 24 weeks or close to it to get ready. Athletes training for shorter events, who are already quite fit, require substantially less time to reach their peak, and when less time is needed, less time generally should be taken. An athlete who is already quite fit and hopes to perform at a peak level in a short event that's 24 weeks away would be well advised to divide the time available into two segments, using the first segment to train at a maintenance level or to prepare for a less important "B" race.

The crucial thing to understand about rate of load increase is that it doesn't offer much latitude. Endurance fitness accrues slowly, even in the most genetically-favored athletes who are highly responsive to training. While you can rush the process of increasing the training load, you can't rush the process of building fitness, which happens on the body's own time, and the only thing you'll achieve by forcing it is overreaching, or perhaps injury. There are exceptions, such as when an athlete has just completed a long race and has another one in a few weeks. In this scenario, the training load will be artificially suppressed as the athlete recovers from the first race, after which the training load can quickly return to the sweet spot because the athlete will not have lost any fitness or training load tolerance in such a short span.

While limited, the latitude coaches do have to manipulate the rate of training load increase is key to developing the individual athlete's fitness. In other words, the training load should not be increased at the same rate for every athlete in every situation. For some athletes, the training load should be increased very slowly, and for other athletes, it can be increased somewhat faster. Here are some general rules for managing the rate of load increase in different circumstances:

HOW TO DETERMINE THE RATE OF INCREASED TRAINING LOAD

QUICK

- The lower an athlete's current training load is, the more quickly it can be increased.

- The more responsive an athlete is to training (i.e., the more quickly they tend to gain fitness), the more quickly their training load can be increased.

- When an athlete's fitness and training load tolerance are "ahead" of their recent training load due to a short interruption or suppression in training, the training load can be increased quickly.

CAUTIOUS

- The higher an athlete's current training load is, the more slowly it should be increased.

- When an athlete is less responsive to training (i.e., they gain fitness more gradually), a gradual increase in training load works best.

- The closer an athlete is to their training load sweet spot, the more slowly the load should be increased.

- Training loads cannot be increased as quickly in running as in other endurance disciplines due to the high-impact nature of the activity.

Tables 4.1, 4.2, and 4.3 present examples of training load rate increases for different situations. The training stress score (TSS) totals given at the end of each week allow you to easily compare rates of load increase across the three examples. (Recall from Chapter 1 that TSS is a measure of the training load imposed by a single workout and serves as the basis for calculating acute and chronic training loads.) All three examples are highly simplified and offered for illustrative purposes only.

TABLE 4.1 LOW RATE OF TRAINING LOAD INCREASE

This three-week progression might be appropriate for an athlete approaching their training load sweet spot. Notice that the load increases come entirely from small upticks in the challenge level of key workouts.

	WEEK 1	WEEK 2	WEEK 3
Monday	EASY WORKOUT 30:00	EASY WORKOUT 30:00	EASY WORKOUT 30:00
Tuesday	MODERATE-INTENSITY WORKOUT 1:10:00 with 35:00 in Zone X–3	MODERATE-INTENSITY WORKOUT 1:15:00 with 40:00 in Zone X–3	MODERATE-INTENSITY WORKOUT 1:20:00 with 45:00 in Zone X–3
Wednesday	EASY WORKOUT 1:00:00	EASY WORKOUT 1:00:00	EASY WORKOUT 1:00:00
Thursday	EASY WORKOUT 1:00:00	EASY WORKOUT 1:00:00	EASY WORKOUT 1:00:00
Friday	HIGH-INTENSITY WORKOUT 55:00 with 20:00 in Zone 4–5	HIGH-INTENSITY WORKOUT 1:00:00 with 22:00 in Zone 4–5	HIGH-INTENSITY WORKOUT 1:00:00 with 24:00 in Zone 4–5
Saturday	EASY WORKOUT 1:00:00	EASY WORKOUT 1:00:00	EASY WORKOUT 1:00:00
Sunday	LONG WORKOUT 2:20:00 with 40:00 in Zone X–3	LONG WORKOUT 2:30:00 with 45:00 in Zone X–3	LONG WORKOUT 2:40:00 with 50:00 in Zone X–3
TOTAL TSS	570	593	616

Less experienced coaches who aren't sure of how to manipulate the rate of training load increase can address this uncertainty in a couple of ways. One is to study the training plans available at 8020endurance.com. These plans have been used with tremendous success by athletes at all levels, so you can trust them to serve as reliable templates for your own plans. A second option is to use the TrainingPeaks Annual Training Plan (ATP) tool, which autogenerates training plans based on a few inputs including start date, end date, initial

TABLE 4.2 **MODERATE RATE OF TRAINING LOAD INCREASE**

This three-week progression might be appropriate for an athlete transitioning from base training to race-specific training. Notice that the load increases come from small upticks in the challenge level of all seven workouts in the week.

	WEEK 1	WEEK 2	WEEK 3
Monday	EASY WORKOUT 20:00	EASY WORKOUT 25:00	EASY WORKOUT 30:00
Tuesday	MODERATE-INTENSITY WORKOUT 45:00 with 15:00 in Zone X–3	MODERATE-INTENSITY WORKOUT 55:00 with 25:00 in Zone X–3	MODERATE-INTENSITY WORKOUT 1:05:00 with 35:00 in Zone X–3
Wednesday	EASY WORKOUT 50:00	EASY WORKOUT 55:00	EASY WORKOUT 1:00:00
Thursday	EASY WORKOUT 50:00	EASY WORKOUT 55:00	EASY WORKOUT 1:00:00
Friday	HIGH-INTENSITY WORKOUT 45:00 with 10:00 in Zone 4–5	HIGH-INTENSITY WORKOUT 50:00 with 14:00 in Zone 4–5	HIGH-INTENSITY WORKOUT 55:00 with 18:00 in Zone 4–5
Saturday	EASY WORKOUT 50:00	EASY WORKOUT 55:00	EASY WORKOUT 1:00:00
Sunday	LONG WORKOUT 1:20:00 with 0:00 in Zone X–3	LONG WORKOUT 1:40:00 with 15:00 in Zone X–3	LONG WORKOUT 2:00:00 with 30:00 in Zone X–3
TOTAL TSS	**405**	**459**	**510**

fitness level, and projected peak training load. Although ATP-generated plans are broader in scope than those built by an experienced coach, the algorithm used to regulate training volume and load over time is grounded in solid science. For this reason, using this tool to create plans for a wide variety of hypothetical athletes is a useful exercise for newer coaches learning the ins and outs of training load manipulation. The next chapter, which addresses the topic of periodization and peaking, will be of some assistance in this regard as well. It includes a number of examples of sensible training load progressions.

TABLE 4.3 **HIGH RATE OF TRAINING LOAD INCREASE**

This three-week progression might be appropriate for an experienced athlete who's highly responsive to training and is returning to race-focused training after an interruption.

	WEEK 1	WEEK 2	WEEK 3
Monday	Rest	Rest	EASY WORKOUT 30:00
Tuesday	MODERATE-INTENSITY WORKOUT 45:00 with 10:00 in Zone X–3	MODERATE-INTENSITY WORKOUT 1:00:00 with 20:00 in Zone X–3	MODERATE-INTENSITY WORKOUT 1:15:00 with 40:00 in Zone X–3
Wednesday	EASY WORKOUT 45:00	EASY WORKOUT 1:00:00	EASY WORKOUT 1:15:00
Thursday	Rest	EASY WORKOUT 45:00	EASY WORKOUT 1:00:00
Friday	HIGH-INTENSITY WORKOUT 45:00 with 10:00 in Zone 4–5	HIGH-INTENSITY WORKOUT 1:00:00 with 16:00 in Zone 4–5	HIGH-INTENSITY WORKOUT 1:15:00 with 24:00 in Zone 4–5
Saturday	EASY WORKOUT 1:00:00	EASY WORKOUT 1:05:00	EASY WORKOUT 1:10:00
Sunday	LONG WORKOUT 1:20:00 with 0:00 in Zone X–3	LONG WORKOUT 2:00:00 with 20:00 in Zone X–3	LONG WORKOUT 2:40:00 with 50:00 in Zone X–3
TOTAL TSS	**329**	**475**	**624**

Account for diminishing returns.

The well-known law of diminishing returns applies to any process wherein each additional investment of time or energy yields a smaller gain than the last. Endurance training is one such process. An athlete who goes from 1 hour of training per week to 2 hours will experience a greater increase in fitness than an athlete who goes from 2 hours to 3 hours, who in turn will experience a greater fitness increase than an athlete who goes from 3 hours to 4 hours, and so on. Eventually, a point is reached at which any additional increase in training load will yield no additional gain in fitness, and any further increases will result in nonfunctional overreaching. As we noted earlier in the chapter, an athlete's training load sweet spot lies just below the level at which load increases cease to yield positive returns.

It's a good idea to consider the law of diminishing returns in managing your athletes' training loads. That's because the risk-reward ratio changes as the load increases, with each increase netting a smaller fitness boost without any compensatory reduction in the risk of overreaching. If endurance training were exempt from the law of diminishing returns, it would always be wise to build an athlete's training load all the way up to their sweet spot. But as the last few steps toward the sweet spot yield very small amounts of additional fitness, there may be times when it's prudent to avoid the associated risk. For example, an athlete who performs shakily in a couple of key workouts five weeks out from an "A" race might need to be content to have their training load capped where it is instead of pushing for the last 1 or 2 percent of untapped fitness.

These are judgment calls. In each instance, you can't evaluate the decision you've made until after the fact, and even then, a firm conclusion is possible only when it's evident you made the *wrong* decision (such as when you push ahead and the athlete overreaches). Being mindful of the law of diminishing returns will help you make the correct decision more often.

Consider other load-related training variables.

Up to this point we have discussed training load as if it were a simple function of volume and intensity. In fact, it is not. In an effort to make the training process more predictable, sports scientists have developed other ways of measuring load that, when considered alongside volume and intensity, paint a fuller picture of its true multidimensionality. Although these concepts have not yet succeeded in making training outcomes more predictable, some have proven useful to coaches in their efforts to manage athletes' training loads more effectively. Here are four specific variables to be mindful of in applying the 80/20 method of endurance training.

Load Density

A week that contains 12 hours of training divided among 10 workouts is not the same as a week that contains the same number of hours divided among 6 workouts. The concept of *load density*—which, in its simplest form, is calculated as weekly training time (i.e., cumulative hours) divided by weekly training frequency (i.e., the number of workouts)—allows us to draw a simple mathematical distinction between the two. The longer the average duration of a week's training sessions becomes, the greater that week's load density is said to be.

Like everything else related to training loads, optimal load density varies between athletes, sports, and circumstances (*principle of specificity*). At the elite level, it tends to be lowest for athletes such as rowers who compete at short distances because they have nothing to gain by performing extremely long endurance workouts that tend to inflate load density. Such athletes are better off doing a lot of shorter workouts. At the other extreme are elite cyclists, who not only must perform multi-hour rides to prepare for multi-hour races but who typically ride their bikes just once a day, keeping the denominator low in the load density equation.

At sub-elite levels of endurance sports, the same general principle applies—athletes training for longer events should have a longer average training session. In practice, however, the most common load density error made by recreational endurance athletes of all types is not training with sufficient frequency. Research has shown that, in general, training frequency has a bigger impact on race performance than workout duration at any given training volume. This is not a blanket rule, but it is something to be conscious of. For example, a runner who is determined to lower their personal best time for the marathon and who currently runs five times and 5.5 hours per week should add one or two runs to their weekly routine, thereby reducing their load density, instead of lengthening their five existing weekly sessions, which would result in a higher load density.

Training Monotony

In the preceding subsection we saw that not all 12-hour training weeks are the same. The concept of training load density allows us to distinguish one 12-hour week from another based on how many workouts these hours are distributed across. But does this mean that all

12-hour weeks with equal numbers of workouts are the same? It does not, and the concept of training monotony shows us why.

Consider two athletes, Jamie and Jesse, who each complete seven workouts and 12 total hours of training in the span of a week. From a certain distance, these two weeks look identical, but a closer inspection might reveal that Jamie's week consists of seven workouts lasting 1 hour and 45 minutes each while Jesse's comprises a half-dozen 1-hour workouts and one 6-hour workout. The regrettable term ***training monotony***, which perhaps ought to be replaced with **training uniformity**, draws a mathematical distinction between these two weeks. Various formulas are used to calculate training monotony, but all serve to quantify how much variation in session length there is within the week.

As with load density, there is no inherently "good" or "bad" degree of training monotony. There are only problematic and unproblematic degrees of training monotony for individual athletes in specific situations. The most prevalent error in this area is a form of excessive session-length variation exhibited by athletes training for longer events. It is not uncommon for runners, triathletes, and others to concentrate too much of their weekly training time in their longer endurance-building sessions. As with load density, however, research suggests that average weekly training time has a bigger impact on performance in longer events than does the duration of the longest individual session. For example, an athlete who trains 12 hours per week but never longer than 3 hours in an individual session is likely to perform better than an athlete who trains 10 hours per week and whose longest individual workouts reach 4 hours in duration.

Keep in mind, though, that the optimal degree of training monotony is situational. To give another example, a certain triathlete's training monotony might be skewed by a 30-minute weekly swim technique session conducted under the supervision of a coach. Given the unique importance of technique in swimming, this workout could very well have a disproportionately large impact on the athlete's performance despite its brevity.

Load Orientation

The term ***load orientation*** is used to denote the specific focus of a workout or block of workouts. The example given at the end of the preceding subsection represents a technique-oriented training session. Other possible load orientations include endurance, aerobic capacity, speed, and strength.

The concept of load orientation is important to consider in coaching athletes with different competitive specializations. One of the dangers of treating chronic training load (CTL) as a stand-in for fitness is that it lumps together all types of fitness. In Chapter 1 it was mentioned that the type of fitness sought by a runner specializing in 1500-meter track races is somewhat different than the type of fitness needed by a runner focused on the marathon. Because elite marathoners typically run more than elite track racers, their peak CTL tends to be slightly higher. It would be a mistake to conclude from this fact that today's elite milers train incorrectly and would get fitter and perform better if they increased their CTL to the level of their marathon-focused peers. Elite middle-distance runners necessarily have a load orientation that is more focused on anaerobic fitness, a highly stressful training stimulus that limits the amount of volume they are able to absorb and depresses their CTL relative to marathoners.

It is simply not valid to compare chronic training loads across competitive specializations. An athlete who goes from BMX racing to multistage road racing will have a different sweet spot for each. Always factor in load orientation, or the type of fitness being sought, when planning and evaluating athletes' training loads (*principle of purpose*). At the same time, understand that the goal is never to prioritize one specific load orientation at the expense of all others. Remember, milers need a certain measure of endurance just as marathoners require a degree of anaerobic fitness.

Subjective Load

Objective metrics such as chronic training load set expectations for how hard a given period of training is likely to seem to the athlete who experiences it. But perceptions don't always match expectations, so there's a need for separate monitoring of subjective training loads. In recognition of this fact, scientists have developed various ways of quantifying the **subjective load**. The simplest of these is session RPE, which is calculated as the product of the athlete's perceived effort rating on a 1–10 scale for the workout as a whole and its duration in minutes. For example, a 48-minute workout that receives a mean intensity rating of 5 from the athlete who did it results in a session RPE of (48 × 5 =) 240.

Tracking subjective loads can be a useful way to learn about how an individual athlete experiences different training stimuli, allowing the coach to better predict how the athlete will be affected by them in the future. It is not particularly useful at a group scale, however, as individual athletes differ in how they perceive workouts of various types. Whether or not you choose to track subjective loads empirically, it is critically important that you communicate with your athletes about how challenging their workouts seem to them. This information is almost always more reliable than objective load data. If a certain workout was objectively easy based on its TSS but subjectively hard according to the athlete who completed it, you can be sure the workout was in fact hard for that athlete, and this information should be taken into account in future planning (*principle of adaptivity*).

Apply the right periodization model.

Any discussion of training load would be incomplete if it failed to linger on the subject of **periodization**, or the art of sequencing workouts to achieve specific training objectives. If training load is the *how* of achieving fitness objectives, periodization is the *why*—the logic behind all of the planning decisions endurance coaches make, including load-related decisions. As such, periodization deserves its own separate chapter. What remains to be said on the subject of regulating training loads will be said in the context of the ensuing examination of periodization.

Periodization
and Peaking

KEY POINTS

⏐ To attain peak endurance fitness an athlete must train in cycles where periods of overloading (i.e., training at higher loads than the athlete is accustomed to) are punctuated by moments of reduced training to permit recovery and adaptation.

⏐ Microcycles should have a fixed duration of seven to ten days and a relatively fixed structure in which workouts of different activity types, intensities, and stress levels are spread out as much as possible.

⏐ Mesocycles, or step cycles, consist of two to three microcycles with incrementally increasing loads followed by a recovery microcycle with reduced load.

⏐ There is more than one effective approach to periodization at the seasonal (or macrocycle) level, but a majority of elite endurance athletes today follow a nonlinear approach, where the training load gradually increases and the most challenging workouts become increasingly race-specific.

⏐ The goal of periodization, regardless of approach, is peak race performance, which requires that the athlete's training load be built up to a brief period of functional overreaching followed by a carefully designed taper period.

There are many factors that endurance coaches must consider in planning athletes' training. Few of these factors are more important than periodization, or the practice of sequencing workouts to achieve specific training objectives. A simple thought experiment shows why.

Imagine you were given a pile of 100 workouts to place on the calendar of an athlete training for an event that's sixteen weeks away. For the sake of argument, let's assume that the quality and appropriateness of the workouts is not in question. All you have to do is deposit these preselected workouts on the calendar. Is this an easy job or a difficult one? Most coaches would say it's a difficult job requiring careful thought. Of the 10^{1000} possible ways to sequence these 100 workouts, only a handful will do the job of developing peak fitness effectively. Anything less than full commitment to the task will result in a bad training plan.

A lot of ink has been spilled on the subject of periodization since Romanian exercise scientist Tudor Bompa introduced the concept in 1963. In the decades that followed, competing systems of periodization vied for superiority. However, recent science (see the resources section for a relevant review paper) indicates that, although some approaches to periodization are better than others, there's more than one approach capable of yielding optimal results. This is why, in the thought experiment just presented, we stated that a *handful* of different sequences would do the job, not just one. The 80/20 Endurance methodology allows individual coaches to select the specific approach to periodization they prefer from among the coequal options available.

This chapter offers flexible parameters for training periodization. These parameters establish a framework within which coaches can perfect their own personal style of workout sequencing. Major sections are devoted to microcycles, mesocycles (or step cycles), and macrocycles, which are the three timescales at which periodization plays out, with different guidelines applying to each. The chapter concludes with a brief but important examination of the phenomenon of peaking, which is the target that all approaches to periodization aim at.

Planning Microcycles

Seven days, or one calendar week, is the default duration of endurance-training microcycles. The practicality of the calendar week is incontestable. We rely on it to set routines for nearly everything we do, from our jobs to our home life to our athletic pursuits. There's an important difference between endurance training and the other things we do on a weekly schedule, however. A book club could meet every six days or every eight days and it would make no practical difference. But physiology operates on a schedule of its own, and endurance training is all about physiology. So, the question must be asked: Is one week the optimal length for a training microcycle? In other words, does a seven-day rotation yield better results than a shorter or longer cycle would?

Most elite athletes have the freedom to train on any schedule. There's nothing that stands in the way of their using shorter or longer microcycles if either is indeed preferable. Nevertheless, a majority of elites train from Monday to Sunday, just like the amateurs. True, there are some elites who practice 8- to 10-day microcycles, and with great success. But the preponderance of evidence suggests that either traditional, 7-day microcycles or slightly longer ones can be made to work for any athlete, at least physiologically, if not practically. This is good news for the majority of endurance athletes who have little choice but to conform to a Monday-to-Sunday routine. They need not fear that in doing so they are artificially limiting their fitness.

What about older athletes, though? Many athletes over the age of forty find that they can't recover from harder workouts as quickly as they once did. Wouldn't these athletes benefit from extending the microcycle by a day or two? In many cases, they would. But there are other ways to accommodate the body's changing needs. One option is to make the athlete's key workouts a little easier so that adequate recovery becomes possible within the constraints of a seven-day cycle. When it's done right, this approach is just as effective as lengthening the week, and it's more practical for many. Also, aging athletes will inevitably arrive at a point where they need to make their key workouts less challenging regardless of how long their microcycles are.

The most popular alternative to a 7-day microcycle is a 9-day microcycle. Athletes who extend the training week to nine days frequently report that the schedule has a comfortable, predictable rhythm. In a 9-day microcycle, harder workouts fall on every third day, ensuring equal recovery time for each, which is harder to achieve on a 7-day cycle. Although

7-day microcycles are optimal for practical reasons, we encourage coaches to be mindful of the *principle of adaptivity*. For athletes who struggle with recovery when trying to fit three harder sessions into a 7-day span, a 9-day microcycle may work best provided they have the flexibility to do longer workouts during the week.

The reason 7-day microcycles work well for most athletes physically, and not just practically, is that seven days happens to be about the right frequency for repeating special training stimuli. Long workouts are the obvious example. An athlete who wishes to build a high level of endurance for a longer race can be confident they will get good results from a plan that features one long workout per week. The same is true of high-intensity training, moderate-intensity training, technique work, and other stimuli. One session every seven days that is focused on any of these stimuli will, in the context of a consistent and progressive training program, suffice to develop the targeted fitness component.

There are many ways in which a 7-day microcycle can be arranged. It is helpful to both coaches and athletes to establish a basic weekly training routine that serves as a template for each week of a given athlete's training. When this is done, the athlete performs the same types of workouts on the same days in every microcycle, and only the specifics change from one week to the next. The advantage of such a framework is that it makes the planning process more efficient and training outcomes more predictable. For example, if resting on Monday, doing harder workouts on Tuesday and Friday, and wrapping up the week with a long workout on Sunday works well for a given athlete one week, then it will probably work well most weeks. There is no need to start with a blank canvas in planning each future week of training.

There are three main factors to consider in devising a weekly routine for an individual athlete: scheduling constraints, training variety, and training frequency. Scheduling constraints are things like school and work that limit when an athlete can train and for how long. In most cases, such constraints are fixed obligations that must be scheduled around. Trying to talk a church deacon out of attending Sunday service so he can use the time for long bike rides instead might not be the best idea!

Training variety relates to the *principle of balance* as discussed in Chapter 1. This principle directs coaches to distribute different types of training as evenly as possible across the microcycle. Specifically, coaches should aim to create separation between workouts of the same type, workouts targeting higher intensities, and hard workouts (a category that encompasses any workout type that results in high levels of fatigue, including long workouts done at low intensity). A certain amount of bunching may sometimes be unavoidable, however, and that's okay. If you coach a triathlete who swims three times a week, and their life schedule requires that a pair of these swims fall on consecutive days, so be it. Just be sure to give those swims different emphases (e.g., speed and endurance).

There are a few special circumstances in which bunching workouts of a particular kind is not only acceptable but desirable. For example, if you are working with a runner who is preparing for the Dopey Challenge, which entails racing a 5K, a 10K, a half marathon, and a marathon on consecutive days, you will probably want to have this runner perform a pair of hard workouts on consecutive days a couple of times during training to prepare them for the unique challenge ahead, even though this practice is normally avoided.

Training frequency is the final determinant of optimal microcycle structure. How many times per week should your athlete row, or strength train, and so on? These questions must be answered before you can set a routine. Consider the athlete's history and established standards for athletes of a given type or level. A runner who has never run more than five times in a week has no business jumping to ten runs per week. As mentioned previously, cyclists are less likely to double up with two shorter workouts in one day than athletes in other endurance disciplines. Don't try to reinvent the wheel, so to speak. It's (almost) always safe to start an athlete at or slightly above a frequency at which they've had prior success, and to use weekly routines that are standard for the category of athlete you're working with. We once again direct you to the training plans available at 8020endurance.com, which serve as useful guides for this element of planning.

The most challenging microcycles to plan are those intended for athletes who train at a high level in multiple disciplines. Experienced competitive triathletes, in particular, have more priorities to balance in a week than just about any other type of athlete. Table 5.1 presents an example of a 7-day routine for a triathlete who swims, cycles, and runs four times per week and strength trains twice per week. The same week is rendered in three different ways to highlight how training is balanced across three separate axes—activity type, intensity, and difficulty.

As you can see, this schedule does a reasonably good job of achieving balance along all three axes. Is it perfect? No, but perfection is not attainable for an athlete trying to balance so many different factors. Are there alternative ways of structuring a microcycle that would

3 VIEWS OF AN EXAMPLE MICROCYCLE

TABLE 5.1A **ACTIVITY TYPE**

MONDAY	TUESDAY	WEDNESDAY	THURSDAY	FRIDAY	SATURDAY	SUNDAY
Easy Swim	High-Intensity Bike	Easy Swim	High-Intensity Run	Strength Training	Long Bike	Long Run
Strength Training	Moderate-Intensity Run	Easy Bike	Moderate-Intensity Bike	High-Intensity Swim	Easy Run	Moderate-Intensity Swim

TABLE 5.1B **INTENSITY**

MONDAY	TUESDAY	WEDNESDAY	THURSDAY	FRIDAY	SATURDAY	SUNDAY
Easy Swim	High-Intensity Bike	Easy Swim	High-Intensity Run	Strength Training	Long Bike	Long Run
Strength Training	Moderate-Intensity Run	Easy Bike	Moderate-Intensity Bike	High-Intensity Swim	Easy Run	Moderate-Intensity Swim

⦿ LOW INTENSITY   ● MODERATE INTENSITY   ●● HIGH INTENSITY

TABLE 5.1C **DIFFICULTY**

MONDAY	TUESDAY	WEDNESDAY	THURSDAY	FRIDAY	SATURDAY	SUNDAY
◇ Easy Swim	◆◆ High-Intensity Bike	◇ Easy Swim	◆◆ High-Intensity Run	Strength Training	◆ Long Bike	◆◆ Long Run
Strength Training	◆◆ Moderate-Intensity Run	◇ Easy Bike	◆◆ Moderate-Intensity Bike	◆ High-Intensity Swim	◇ Easy Run	◆◆ Moderate-Intensity Swim

◇ NO HARD WORKOUTS   ◆ 1 HARD WORKOUT   ◆◆ 2 HARD WORKOUTS work just as well? Yes. For example, the bunching of moderate- and high-intensity workouts on Tuesday and Thursday could be reduced by decreasing the number of days with two hard workouts. However, this would reduce or even eliminate days with no hard workouts. There's always a trade-off.

Here are some additional tips for planning microcycles:

Aiming for an approximate 80/20 intensity balance helps with decisions about which types of workouts to slot into the general microcycle framework and how long they should be. For athletes who train at high frequency and volume, like the one in the example above, you often need to include some efforts at moderate or high intensity within their long workouts to achieve an 80/20 balance, which is fine given that long workouts are classified as hard regardless.

Keep in mind that not all hard workouts need to be equally hard. One way to maintain balance within a microcycle is to include lighter workouts at moderate or high intensity as needed. For example, a highly challenging Tuesday tempo run might be followed by a Wednesday ride that features a handful of short, high-intensity efforts sprinkled throughout an otherwise low-intensity spin.

It's possible to improve the overall balance of an athlete's training by rotating among two or three slightly different microcycles over the course of a mesocycle. For example, you could alternate the order of the long ride and long run from week to week so the athlete isn't always doing the run with tired legs.

Planning Step Cycles (Mesocycles)

The key difference between microcycles and mesocycles (or step cycles, as we will call them) is training load variation. Step cycles are the primary instrument through which coaches apply the *principle of progression* in planning athletes' training. We know that training loads must increase over time for fitness to increase. But the proper timescale for increasing the training load is week by week, not day by day, because fatigue accumulates faster than fitness builds. Any athlete who tried to train harder each day over the course of a microcycle would be too fatigued going into their hardest workouts at the end of the week to get much out of them. Increasing the training load for two to three weeks at a time, however, is very doable, and that's why most elite endurance athletes do it.

In a typical step cycle, the first week features a training load that is slightly greater than that of the heaviest week of the preceding step cycle, the second week is heavier still, and the third week is a recovery (or "down") week, where the training load is lightened just enough to enable the athlete to emerge ready to take on a microcycle that's slightly more challenging than the last. A 4-week cycle simply extends this progression to three "up" weeks for every down week.

Three-week cycles are a good default because they can be made to work well for almost any athlete. All it requires is that the training load be fine-tuned to ensure the athlete *needs* a recovery week every third week. And recovery weeks themselves can be fine-tuned—made light enough to leave the athlete ready to absorb harder training but no lighter than necessary. The term "recovery week" implies a sharp reduction in training load, but there's no reason a down week can't be marginally less challenging than an up week, if need be. A small decrease in load is often sufficient for less-fit athletes who aren't able to train at particularly high loads during their up weeks, as well as for athletes at the other extreme, who, by virtue of their fitness and experience, can tolerate very high loads and would probably need to go longer between recovery weeks if the load were sharply reduced within them. Similar methods of load tuning can be used to make 4-week step cycles a good fit for most athletes. For example, the week-to-week training load increases in up weeks can be made very small to minimize the risk of overreaching between down weeks. Four-week step cycles tend to be preferred by more experienced, competitive, and younger athletes, and there is no reason not to accommodate this preference in such athletes if they have a proven ability to tolerate them.

Table 5.2 presents an example of a 3-week step cycle for a cyclist preparing for a long-distance gravel race. As you can see, a fixed weekly structure is held across the step cycle. Progression is achieved entirely through increases in the difficulty level (measured as training stress score) of the key workouts on the second, fifth, and seventh days of each week. Total training time and cumulative training stress increase from Week 1 to Week 2 and drop to their lowest level in Week 3, but the intensity balance remains constant at 80/20 in all three weeks. If Week 4 were shown, the cumulative TSS would be slightly greater than in Week 2.

Like the example microcycle given in the previous section, this step cycle is intended as illustration only. A different example might have included recovery rides on Day 1 of Weeks 1 and 2 and a rest day in Week 3 only, and a third might have featured slight changes in the durations of the easy rides from week to week. In short, there is more than one way to plan a step cycle that conforms to general best practices.

Organizing the training process in step cycles is not always necessary. Whenever an athlete is training at a maintenance level (as during the off-season), where the load is never greater than the athlete could sustain indefinitely, there is no need to distinguish between

TABLE 5.2 **EXAMPLE OF A 3-WEEK STEP CYCLE**

	WEEK 1	**WEEK 2**	**WEEK 3**
Monday	Rest	Rest	Rest
Tuesday	TEMPO RIDE 1:10:00 with 30:00 in Zone 3	CRITICAL POWER RIDE 1:20:00 with 25:00 in Zone Y	CRUISE INTERVALS RIDE 1:00:00 with 20:00 in Zone 3
Wednesday	EASY RIDE 1:00:00 in Zone 2	EASY RIDE 1:00:00 in Zone 2	EASY RIDE 1:00:00 in Zone 2
Thursday	EASY RIDE 1:00:00 in Zone 2	EASY RIDE 1:00:00 in Zone 2	EASY RIDE 1:00:00 in Zone 2
Friday	SPEED INTERVALS RIDE 1:00:00 with 20:00 in Zone 5	LACTATE INTERVALS RIDE 1:10:00 with 25:00 in Zone 4	MIXED INTERVALS RIDE 50:00 with 15:00 in Zones 4 and 5
Saturday	EASY RIDE 1:00:00 in Zone 2	EASY RIDE 1:00:00 in Zone 2	EASY RIDE 1:00:00 in Zone 2
Sunday	LONG GRAVEL RIDE 3:00:00 with 50:00 in Zone X	LONG GRAVEL RIDE 3:20:00 with 55:00 in Zone X	LONG GRAVEL RIDE 2:00:00 with 45:00 in Zone X
TOTAL TIME	**8:10:00**	**8:50:00**	**6:50:00**
Total TSS	532	555	418
Intensity Balance	80/20	80/20	80/20

up weeks and down weeks. Remember, though, that step cycles serve not only to help coaches vary the training load in a systematic way but also to ensure that the athlete's training is properly balanced. Step cycles remain useful for this purpose even when an athlete is training at a maintenance level. For instance, it might be appropriate for an athlete who's currently in maintenance training to perform a hill repetitions workout of some kind every three weeks. In this case, planning in step cycles makes sense even though the athlete is not training hard enough to need recovery weeks.

There are legitimate methods of mesocycle planning other than step cycles. Among them is **block periodization**, in which multiweek blocks of training that feature a lot of volume and little or no work at higher intensities are interspersed with shorter blocks containing concentrated work at higher intensities and less overall volume. Studies indicate that this approach—which applies an 80/20 intensity balance on a mesocycle level, though not on the microcycle level—can be quite effective. We mention this particular example only to underscore the point that there is more than one good way to plan mesocycles, and it's okay for you as a coach to take advantage of this flexibility in developing your own approach. The 3-week step cycle method we've concentrated on in this section is considered the 80/20 Endurance standard and a solid starting point for any coach.

Planning Macrocycles

A macrocycle is a period of training that is focused on preparing the athlete for a single peak performance. A classic macrocycle begins on the day the athlete starts to actively build fitness for an "A" race and ends with that race. There are three basic types of macrocycles: linear, nonlinear, and acyclic.

Linear Macrocycles

A **linear macrocycle** is made up of distinct phases, each emphasizing a specific component of fitness. The most familiar linear periodization model begins with an aerobic base phase emphasizing low-intensity work and building endurance then transitions to a strength phase emphasizing moderate-intensity efforts and working against resistance (e.g., hills), a speed phase prioritizing (you guessed it) speed development, and a racing phase focused on recovery and sharpening for competition. Strict linear periodization is not widely practiced today.

Nonlinear Macrocycles

In a ***nonlinear macrocycle***, the evolution of training priorities is more fluid. All components of endurance fitness are always being worked on, only the emphasis changes. Progress toward peak race fitness is achieved by gradually increasing the overall training load and by making the hardest individual workouts more and more race-specific. The particular types of workouts prioritized at a given time are determined by the nature of the race the athlete is preparing for (*principle of specificity*) and by the athlete's location within the macrocycle. Tables 5.3–5.7 demonstrate the logic to apply in planning nonlinear macrocycles.

Once again, we willingly confess that these tables oversimplify things a bit. Are races lasting 31 minutes really categorically different from races lasting 29 minutes? Unlikely. Are there truly four distinct periods of training in a nonlinear macrocycle? No. As mentioned above, training priorities evolve fluidly over time in nonlinear periodization. Are Zone 4

EVOLUTION OF TRAINING PRIORITIES

TABLE 5.3 **RACES LASTING 2–6 MINUTES**

	PHASE I	PHASE II	PHASE III	PHASE IV
1	Long Zone 2 Workout	Zone 3 Tempos	Zone 4 Intervals	Zone 5 Intervals
2	Zone 3 Tempo	Zone 5 Intervals	Zone 5 Intervals	Zone 4 Intervals
3	Zone 5 Intervals	Long Zone 2 Workout	Zone 3 Tempo	Zone 3 Tempo
4	Zone 4 Intervals	Zone 4 Intervals	Long Zone 2 Workout	Long Zone 2 Workout
5	Zone X Steady State	Zone X Steady State	Zone X Steady State	Zone X Steady State

TABLE 5.4 **RACES LASTING 6–30 MINUTES**

	PHASE I	PHASE II	PHASE III	PHASE IV
1	Long Zone 2 Workout	Zone 5 Intervals	Zone 3 Tempo	Zone 4 Intervals
2	Zone 5 Intervals	Zone X Steady State	Zone 4 Intervals	Zone 3 Tempo
3	Zone 3 Tempo	Zone 4 Intervals	Zone 5 Intervals	Zone 5 Intervals
4	Zone 4 Intervals	Zone 3 Tempo	Zone X Steady State	Zone X Steady State
5	Zone X Steady State	Long Zone 2 Workout	Long Zone 2 Workout	Long Zone 2 Workout

TABLE 5.5 **RACES LASTING 30–90 MINUTES**

	PHASE I	PHASE II	PHASE III	PHASE IV
1	Long Zone 2 Workout	Zone 5 Intervals	Zone 4 Intervals	Zone 3 Tempo
2	Zone 5 Intervals	Long Zone 2 Workout	Zone 3 Tempo	Zone X Steady State
3	Zone 4 Intervals	Zone 4 Intervals	Zone X Steady State	Zone 4 Intervals
4	Zone 3 Tempo	Zone 3 Tempo	Long Zone 2 Workout	Long Zone 2 Workout
5	Zone X Steady State	Zone X Steady State	Zone 5 Intervals	Zone 5 Intervals

TABLE 5.6 **RACES LASTING 1.5–3 HOURS**

	PHASE I	PHASE II	PHASE III	PHASE IV
1	Long Zone 2 Workout	Zone 4 Intervals	Zone 3 Tempo	Zone X Steady State
2	Zone 5 Intervals	Long Zone 2 Workout	Zone X Steady State	Long Zone 2 Workout
3	Zone 4 Intervals	Zone 3 Tempo	Long Zone 2 Workout	Zone 3 Tempo
4	Zone 3 Tempo	Zone X Steady State	Zone 4 Intervals	Zone 4 Intervals
5	Zone X Steady State	Zone 5 Intervals	Zone 5 Intervals	Zone 5 Intervals

TABLE 5.7 **RACES LASTING 3+ HOURS**

	PHASE I	PHASE II	PHASE III	PHASE IV
1	Long Zone 2 Workout	Zone 3 Tempo	Long Zone 2 Workout	Long Zone 2 Workout
2	Zone 5 Intervals	Zone 4 Intervals	Zone 3 Tempo	Zone X Steady State
3	Zone 4 Intervals	Long Zone 2 Workout	Zone X Steady State	Zone 3 Tempo
4	Zone 3 Tempo	Zone X Steady State	Zone 4 Intervals	Zone 4 Intervals
5	Zone X Steady State	Zone 5 Intervals	Zone 5 Intervals	Zone 5 Intervals

intervals unquestionably the third-highest training priority in the second phase of a nonlinear microcycle ending in a race lasting between 30 and 90 minutes? Again, no. Yet, despite the hedging involved, we believe these four tables constitute a helpful tool for organizing your thinking on the subject of nonlinear periodization.

To put the tables to practical use, you must first understand what is meant by the ordinal rankings of workout types. They are *not* intended to dictate how much time ought to be devoted to a given training type. Instead these rankings indicate 1) how challenging each workout type should be relative to other workout types, and 2) the order in which workout types should be focused on, especially in the event that the athlete cannot complete all of the planned workouts in a particular period of training. For example, "Long Zone 2 Workout" is ranked first in Phase III of training for macrocycles ending with a race lasting more than 3 hours. This means that the most challenging workout in this period should be a long Zone 2 workout, and that workouts of this type should be the last ones an athlete skips at this point of the season.

Of course, what's challenging for one athlete is not necessarily challenging for another. When planning workouts, consider not only the priority level of the particular fitness component addressed by the workout but also the fitness level of the athlete (*principle of individualization*). For instance, how challenging is a tempo workout featuring 30 minutes of work in Zone 3? Well, for an advanced athlete who has a lot of practice with extended efforts at moderate intensity, this workout might be appropriate at a time when Zone 3 is the *lowest* fitness priority, whereas for a less experienced athlete with less practice the same workout might be appropriate when Zone 3 is the *highest* priority.

Although training loads are not represented in the table, they should be understood to increase in each phase for all race distances except races lasting less than 6 minutes. As we saw in Chapter 4, commonly used training load metrics are biased toward high volume, and athletes focused on the shortest endurance events must often reduce their volume in the later phases in order to be able to tolerate the highly challenging race-specific workouts that are prioritized within them.

Also keep in mind that as the training load increases, fitness increases. As fitness increases, athletes can handle bigger workouts of all kinds. Let's go back to our example of a tempo workout featuring 30 minutes of work in Zone 3. It's conceivable that this workout could be used as a first-priority workout in the early part of a macrocycle and as a third-priority workout in a later part of the macrocycle, when the athlete is fitter and the same workout is no longer as challenging as it was previously.

Finally, you may have noticed that the rankings look very similar across all race durations in Phase I and diverge from there. This pattern is a hallmark of nonlinear periodization: The macrocycle starts with a period of general fitness development that is equally suitable for athletes across specializations and then becomes increasingly specific to the targeted race type. Indeed, this initial period is often referred to as the general preparation phase, while the next period is labeled the specific phase. The main purpose of the early weeks of a macrocycle is to build the capacity to handle the harder and increasingly race-specific training to come. This is best done by focusing on building up the overall volume of training, and the most practical way to build overall volume is by prioritizing gentle Zone 2 training. For most race distances, Zone 5 intervals are the second priority in this period because it is the least race-specific fitness component and because small amounts of Zone 5 work go a long way toward increasing overall training tolerance.

Acyclic Macrocycles

In recent decades, a type of nonlinear macrocycle that we call *acyclic* has gained traction in certain segments of the elite stratum of endurance sports. Especially popular among athletes who race frequently, **acyclic periodization** entails training at a high but sustainable baseline level throughout the macrocycle. This allows athletes to sharpen up quickly for races and then return to baseline after a short recovery period. When planned and executed skillfully, this approach gives athletes the flexibility to compete often at or near peak fitness without undue risk of overreaching. It tends to work well for team athletes, including high school and college cross country runners, who compete multiple times over the course of a season, as well as for triathletes who specialize in short-course events and other seasonal racers. Acyclic periodization has also been used successfully by ultrarunners and other athletes who, despite racing less frequently, prefer this "always ready" way of training.

The key to success with acyclic periodization is finding the right baseline for the individual athlete. Set it too high and the athlete will overreach and require a break at an inopportune time. Set it too low and the athlete will be forced to race at a suboptimal level of fitness. It often takes a bit of experimentation to find the highest training load that a given athlete can sustain almost indefinitely (*principle of adaptivity*). A good way to start the process is by thinking about how you would have the athlete train six or seven weeks out from an "A" race in a traditional macrocycle, or just before the athlete arrives at their training load sweet spot. Chances are pretty good the athlete will be able to sustain this level of training for an extended period of time, and, by definition, it puts them in a position where they're never more than a few weeks away from being 100 percent race-ready.

The post-race period plays a pivotal role in making acyclic periodization work. At this time, the training load must be reduced just enough to enable the athlete to resume baseline training without risk of overreaching, but not so much that the athlete loses significant fitness and the capacity to tolerate baseline training. The specific degree and length of the training reduction will need to vary depending on the nature and length of the race and the training load that preceded it. Longer races and higher loads require greater and longer reductions, and the athlete's individual capacity to recover will need to be taken into account as well.

A *word of caution:* Although a well-planned acyclic macrocycle will allow the athlete to achieve a greater number of peak performances over a longer period of time as compared to a traditional macrocycle, it will not allow the athlete to prolong the macrocycle indefinitely. Eventually, the athlete will need to take a break from intensive training, not merely for physical reasons but also for psychological reasons. Even the acyclic approach to periodization requires an investment of emotional resources that is not sustainable year-round, as established by the *principle of cyclicality*.

Peaking and Tapering

As we have seen, there are a number of different approaches to periodization. The thing that should not be overlooked in discussing what distinguishes one from another is the fact that all of them share a common objective, which is to enable athletes to achieve a peak performance in their next important race (*principle of purpose*).

A peak performance is simply a level of performance that is exceptional for a given athlete and made possible by three conditions:

1. **A progressive training process** that culminates in a brief period of functional overreaching where the athlete is training at a level that, although unsustainable, does not exceed their body's capacity to adapt beneficially.
2. **A taper**, which is a short phase where the training load is sharply reduced to enable the body to fully recover from and adapt to the peak training just completed.
3. **The conscious expectation** of achieving a peak performance in an upcoming race. Athletes must believe they're going to perform at an exceptional level to do so.

Tapering methods have been intensively studied, and while there is no compelling evidence that one particular method is best, there are a handful of proven guidelines that all tapers should obey.

GUIDELINES FOR TAPERS

The **DURATION** of the taper should be proportional to the peak training load. For casual athletes, who peak at relatively modest training loads, a taper lasting only a few days might be optimal. Elite athletes, who peak at very high training loads, may need to begin tapering three to four weeks before their race to achieve a peak performance.

LOW-INTENSITY TRAINING should be reduced more sharply than high-intensity training within the taper. Studies have shown that a combination of sharply reduced low-intensity training and moderately reduced high-intensity training produces the biggest changes in myocellular properties linked to peak performance.

Independent of peak training load, **SHORT RACES** lasting only a few minutes require longer tapers. This is because it takes longer for the body to fully recover from and adapt to the high-intensity, strength, and power training that are emphasized in programs targeting short events.

The taper should be disciplined, meaning that once the athlete begins to reduce their training load, they continue to do so all the way to race day.

The taper should be tailored to the individual. Not all athletes respond the same way to the same taper. It may take some time to find the optimal tapering protocol for each athlete you work with.

SIMPLE RULES FOR PERIODIZATION

The practice of sequencing workouts can seem more complicated than it really is, especially for beginning coaches. Behind the polysyllabic terminology, effective periodization comes down to a few simple rules:

- Balance training within the week.
- Increase training load gradually from week to week, except in every third or fourth week when it should be reduced to prevent fatigue from accumulating to unacceptably high levels.

- Emphasize types of training that are increasingly race-specific as competition draws near.
- Plan for the training process to culminate in a brief period of functional overreaching, or training at the sweet spot of training load, followed by a short pre-race taper.

If the plans you create for athletes do these things, success will follow.

Keeping Athletes on Track

⟋ Problems are bound to arise in endurance training. Coaches have a pivotal role in helping athletes identify and overcome problems so they can stay on track toward their goals.

⟋ To minimize the impact of unforeseen problems on an athlete's progress, coaches must monitor relevant information to evaluate how things are going and manage the plan for the athlete, making decisions based on the information taken in.

⟋ It's common for coaches to be misled as a result of overanalyzing information, paying too much attention to the wrong kinds of data, and measurement bias (i.e., placing too much importance on certain training metrics).

⟋ Coaches must modify subsequent training in targeted ways to correct the problem or limit its impact, departing from the original plan as much as necessary but no more.

The *principle of adaptivity* exists because the training process never goes entirely as expected. No matter how much care you put into planning an athlete's training, problems will inevitably arise in its execution. What then? Having gotten the athlete on track to achieve their next big goal through appropriate planning, how do you adapt in order to keep them on track in the face of obstacles such as injury and lapses in motivation? The two best practices in this area of coaching are *monitoring* and *managing*, which together enable coaches to apply the adaptivity principle in a way that minimizes the impact of problems on athlete progression.

The type of monitoring that coaches do for their athletes entails taking in relevant information to better evaluate how things are going. This is not unlike the type of monitoring that loss prevention agents do in retail stores. A loss prevention agent is not interested in law-abiding customers who are doing what shoppers are expected to do. Rather, they are interested in, and constantly looking out for, thieves. Similarly, as a coach, you are less interested in workouts that go well than in workouts that don't. After all, a good workout is merely a fulfillment of expectations. Except in cases where you learn something that is useful toward future planning, a good workout requires only the passive response of sticking with the plan. But a bad workout, or a rough patch in training, signals a problem, and problems seldom fix themselves. Whether it's a small problem, such as difficulty in adjusting to the arrival of summer weather conditions, or a big one, such as a bone stress reaction, the coach has a responsibility to take active measures to keep the athlete on track in their training, or, if it's too late for that, to get them back on track. In other words, the coach needs to make decisions based on the information taken in, effectively managing the athlete's problem.

The purpose of this chapter is to provide a clear conceptual framework you can use to help athletes stay on track. But before we delve into how a coach identifies problems (monitors the training process) and addresses problems (manages the training process), we must first define what it means to be on track or off track in endurance training, and this requires a discussion of goal setting.

Goal Setting

Goals provide the standard by which coaches and athletes judge how well the training process is going. In much the same way you need to know a train's destination and schedule to know whether it is on track for a timely arrival, you and your athletes need to have specific goals in place before you can meaningfully evaluate how the training process is going. The goals that endurance athletes pursue can be categorized as process goals, outcome goals, or ultimate ambitions. We'll tackle these in reverse chronological order, starting with the most long-term goals, ultimate ambitions.

Ultimate Ambitions

Not all athletes are dreamers, but if you're a dreamer yourself, or you've worked with this type of athlete, you know that dreams tend to reflect the athlete's passion more than their potential. Consider the millions of athletes who have been inspired to take up a sport by seeing it performed at the highest level in the Olympic Games. Very few of these athletes had a realistic chance of reaching the Olympics, but seeing athletes compete in this rarefied forum ignited a new passion to achieve something significant.

Coaches should support their athletes' dreams (i.e., ultimate ambitions) no matter how outlandish they may seem and avoid offering an opinion on how realistic they are. We say this for several reasons.

Reality speaks for itself. If an athlete's ultimate ambition is beyond their reach, they will discover it for themselves in due time. There's simply no need for coaches to proactively crush their athletes' dreams. Let reality do that.

No coach really knows how much improvement an athlete is capable of. We've all heard stories of athletes who were told by a coach that they would never amount to anything before going on to achieve greatness, fueled in part by a desire to prove the coach wrong. Do you want to be that coach—to become famous for pouring cold water on the dreams of an athlete who ultimately achieves them, not because of you but in spite of you? We'll answer that one for you: No, you do not.

Expectations are self-fulfilling. Studies have shown that coaches' perceptions of athletes' abilities and potential for improvement influence their effort and performance, for better or worse. For this reason, you should not only avoid telling an athlete they can't achieve an ultimate ambition but avoid even thinking it.

Effective coaches avoid putting themselves in a position where they're telling an athlete what they can't do. It's important that your athletes look at you as someone who helps them see what *is* possible, not what isn't. Granted, there are some instances when using the "C" word with an athlete is necessary. For example, if you have an athlete who is in a rush to attempt their first 100-mile ultramarathon and you think they're just not ready, you should tell them. But in doing so, make it clear to the athlete that you're not saying you don't believe they can run 100 miles—you're merely saying they need more time to prepare. Always use the lightest touch you can when articulating your beliefs about an athlete's limitations.

To be clear, we're not saying you should lie by telling athletes you believe they can achieve ultimate ambitions when you really don't; we're merely advising you to refrain from explicitly saying they can't. In the language of politics, we're suggesting you abstain from voting rather than voting yea or nay on such matters. Don't be evasive, however, as athletes are likely to interpret such behavior negatively. Simply explain that, for the reasons given here, you prefer not to offer an opinion on how far athletes can eventually get.

Now, if you happen to believe that a particular athlete is already on their way toward achieving their ultimate ambition, go ahead and sketch out a plan. In these cases, the dream is really just another outcome goal. In all other cases, encourage the athlete to hold their dream in their heart while keeping their eyes focused on the next step.

Another reason to withhold your opinion on the attainability of ultimate ambitions is that, except in rare cases, it does no harm for athletes to chase ultimate ambitions that are beyond their reach. To the contrary, dreams are powerful motivators. More often than not, athletes who pursue unrealistic dreams achieve more than they would have achieved without them, despite falling short of their ultimate ambitions. For these athletes, the dream has served its true purpose, which is to stretch them beyond their present limits and toward the realization of their full potential. Ultimate ambitions become harmful only when athletes get ahead of themselves, rushing a process that can't be rushed. An athlete's *next* big goal should always be one that is realistic given their current level of development.

Finally, whereas keeping quiet when an athlete articulates an unrealistic ultimate ambition does not harm them, telling an athlete that you don't believe they can realize their athletic dreams does them no good. There is no benefit to the athlete whatsoever, unless you count it as beneficial to spare an athlete from possible future disappointment by whacking them with definite present disappointment.

Outcome Goals

Outcome goals have to do with an athlete's performance in workouts and races. These goals exist on a hierarchy of importance. At the top of the hierarchy are the primary performance goals athletes set for races. An appropriate goal of this kind is one that is judged to be difficult, but not impossible, for the athlete to achieve based on available information. Unlike ultimate ambitions, which coaches should not interfere with, primary performance goals should be decided upon collaboratively between athletes and coaches. Not every athlete sets good primary performance goals on their own. Your role here is to help your athletes set goals that are just barely reachable. The reason is simple: Studies have shown that athletes perform better when given this type of goal than they do when given harder or easier goals.

The problem with outcome goals is that, in many cases, they depend on factors that are beyond an athlete's control, and it is unwise to define success in a way that requires luck. For example, an athlete whose primary performance goal is to qualify for the Ironman 70.3 World Championship could have the race of their life yet miss out on qualifying because a recently retired professional triathlete, now competing as an amateur, shows up to compete in the same age group. It makes no sense to label this performance a failure.

Some athletes try to mitigate their dependence on factors beyond their control by setting easier-to-achieve secondary and tertiary goals to fall back on in the event that their primary performance goal turns out to be impossible to achieve, perhaps due to poor weather or an equipment malfunction (or a ringer showing up to compete in their age division). There's nothing wrong with this practice, but even these softer outcome goals involve some degree of external dependency. The best fix for the inherent weakness of outcome goals is to complement them with process goals, which define success in ways that are entirely within the athlete's control. We will discuss process goals next, and we'll come back to them in Chapter 9.

The most sensible starting point for setting outcome goals is past performance. If you're coaching a runner who just completed their fifth marathon with a personal best (PB) time of 3:33:14, and you have reason to believe the athlete is capable of further improvement, the two of you might choose to start the next marathon cycle with the goal of breaking 3:30:00. This goal should be revisited as the training cycle unfolds, and revised as necessary based on the athlete's progress. Even here, though, past performance is the best guide. If the athlete is blowing away the times they ran in certain key workouts prior to setting their PB, consider adjusting their goal time downward. But if they're struggling to match their prior marks, it's probably best to make the goal more conservative.

You now see that the link between outcome goals and your assessments of how the training process is going functions in both directions. On the one hand, outcome goals set the standard by which coaches assess how training is going, while on the other hand, assessments of how the training process is going are useful in adjusting outcome goals appropriately. When an athlete is no longer on track to achieve a goal that was realistic at the time it was set, you know the training process is not going as well as it should. But until and unless the underlying problem is identified and fixed, setting the athlete back on track, a goal revision must be considered. It does an athlete no good to continue to pursue a goal that has become unrealistic.

Some workouts are more useful than others in judging whether an athlete is on track toward a race outcome goal. Generally speaking, the more challenging the workout is, the more it will tell you about how an athlete is likely to perform in an upcoming competition. The reason is that, like races, hard workouts indicate an athlete's limits, whereas easier workouts do not. Whenever an athlete performs a limit-testing workout, use the result to estimate how the athlete would have performed in their upcoming race had they done the race today, instead of their workout. Then estimate how much the athlete is likely to improve given the amount of time they have to get fitter before they actually race. This is not an exact science, but it is something every coach learns to do over time.

You can accelerate this learning process by using certain types of workouts repeatedly in training for specific races. For example, with runners training for 10K races, you might lace the macrocycle with a series of critical velocity workouts sequenced in order of increasing difficulty. Do this with a handful of athletes and you will soon develop a good feel for the mathematical relationship between performance in these workouts and actual 10K race performance.

Process Goals

Process goals are the most important type of goal an athlete can have, and they are also the most underutilized. Examples of process goals include making sure the last repetition is the fastest one in interval workouts, doing at least 10 minutes of mobility work at least three times per week, and keeping heart rate below 135 bpm in easy workouts. What do all of these examples have in common? They serve as ways to keep athletes focused on what matters most in endurance training, which is doing a lot of little things right consistently. Outcome goals have more sizzle, but research has shown that well-chosen process goals yield better outcomes by making athletes more adherent to training prescriptions, reducing anxiety, and increasing training enjoyment.

To serve their purpose, process goals must be relevant to the desired outcome and controllable by the athlete. You can ensure that process goals are relevant by choosing ones that address a particular problem or limiter an athlete has. The goal of making sure the last repetition is the fastest one in interval workouts, for example, is a good choice for an athlete who has a bad habit of blowing workouts through over-aggressive pacing. Finding small ways to reward athletes for adherence to process goals can aid adherence by lending them a bit of the sizzle of outcome goals. For example, you can leverage the *principle of enjoyment* by gamifying an athlete's goal of keeping their heart rate below 135 bpm in easy workouts, challenging the athlete to hit an exact average heart rate (e.g., 132 bpm) in a particular easy session and rewarding them in some small way if they pull it off.

Monitoring and Assessment

Now that we have established what it means to be on or off track in training, let's talk about what it takes to keep athletes on track. The first thing it takes is routine monitoring and assessment of their training. There are two basic categories of information you'll want to pay attention to in this process: objective data and subjective reports. Objective data consists of physiological and performance measurements, while subjective reports are communications from athletes about how they are experiencing their training.

Objective Data

The two most common mistakes that coaches make in monitoring objective data are over-analyzing and measurement bias. The advent of wearable devices and other sports tracking technologies has greatly increased the variety of metrics available to coaches and athletes. Many of these metrics have some potential value, but very few can be considered essential to keeping athletes on track, and paying attention to too many metrics at once can lead to so-called analysis paralysis. Research has shown that athletes perform worse in time trials when they are exposed to too many different kinds of performance data during them, and something similar is true of coaches undertaking post-workout data analysis. Select the most relevant metrics to monitor and tune out the rest.

The only metrics that are truly essential to monitor are basic load measures including volume and intensity. As a coach, you need to have reliable information about how much athletes are training (time, distance) and how hard they are training (pace, power, heart rate). All other metrics are nonessential, and we know this because there are plenty of coaches who monitor nothing else besides volume and intensity and whose athletes nevertheless compete and win at the highest level.

Certain nonessential metrics can be quite useful, however. *Heart rate variability* (HRV) is one example of a nonessential metric that can be a valuable supplement to load metrics because it provides a window into how the athlete's body is responding to the load. Whereas training load is an input and performance an output, heart rate variability is a biometric indicator, an organic link between training inputs and performance outputs. As such, HRV doesn't merely highlight something you're already measuring by other means but fills a gap in the picture.

A given training metric can offer value by providing information that is descriptive, diagnostic, predictive, or prescriptive. When considering whether to track a certain metric with athletes, think about what insight the metric offers and how it should be used to ensure its potential value is actualized. *Descriptive data* supplies information about what happens during a workout, an example being elevation gain. To provide actual descriptive value, the data source must be both pertinent and reliable. *Diagnostic data* tells you why something happens. For example, a low blood glucose reading from a continuous glucose monitor might explain why an athlete felt lethargic in a workout.

There are numerous metrics with legitimate descriptive and diagnostic value to endurance coaches. The same cannot be said with respect to predictive and prescriptive value. **Predictive data** supplies information about what will happen in the future. An example of this is TrainingPeaks's training stress balance (TSB), a measure of the relationship between acute and chronic training loads, which can be used to predict an athlete's readiness to perform. **Prescriptive data** supplies information on how to make a desired outcome happen. An example of this is waking HRV, an indicator of an athlete's fatigue level that is used by many coaches and athletes to inform decisions on how hard to train that day.

There is broad agreement among the best minds in endurance coaching and sports data analytics today that the newer and fancier technologies put forward thus far for predictive and prescriptive use in training are no match for traditional, low-tech sources of predictive and prescriptive information. At this time there is simply no better basis for predicting the sort of training an athlete will most benefit from doing next than the combination of:

1. information about the athlet's recent training,
2. general knowledge of endurance training principles, and
3. subjective reports from the athlete.

For example, if you know an athlete has trained more lightly than usual the past ten days, and you know that a short-term reduction in training load tends to reduce fatigue without reducing fitness in athletes (*principle of cyclicality*), and if the athlete tells you they're feeling good, you know they're ready to train hard, regardless of what the data from some wearable device says.

We're not suggesting that fancier forms of data should never be used predictively or prescriptively. What we are suggesting is that, to the extent that you rely on an advanced data source to inform your coaching decisions, you'd better understand its flaws and limitations. To actualize the latent value in any training metric—whether it be descriptive, diagnostic, predictive, or prescriptive—a coach must know how to interpret and contextualize the data it supplies. HRV and other biometrics that more and more coaches are choosing to monitor don't function like fire alarms, communicating a simple or obvious message, but instead require a degree of interpretation based on context. A fire alarm tells you what to do, in no uncertain terms. Biometric data should never tell any coach what to do. A good rule of thumb is this: Never monitor a metric that you do not feel in total command of. When you are in command of a metric such as HRV, it *informs* your decisions, but it does not make your decisions.

At the end of the day, all you're really trying to do when analyzing an athlete's workout data is to determine whether or not the workout went as expected. If it did, as most workouts do, you know it's safe to stay the course. And if it didn't, your job is to try to figure out why and adjust the program as necessary. When an athlete completes a workout as prescribed, performs at about the level expected, and does not struggle, check the box and move on. There is no need to get lost in the weeds of empirical data.

In fact, there is more than one good reason *not* to study the numbers too closely in analyzing workouts. Data-obsessed coaches raise a lot of false alarms. No data source is perfect, and again, all of them require interpretation. In much the same way that a healthy person who is subjected to every known medical test is bound to discover something to worry about unnecessarily, a coach who routinely pays attention to the minutiae of a wide variety of training metrics is bound to see problems that aren't real problems but "measurement problems"—i.e., problems that wouldn't exist if the device that detected them didn't exist. Again, we're not advocating inattention, but merely encouraging a big-picture focus and a loose hold on the reins of athlete monitoring.

Scientists use the term "coarse-graining" to refer to the practice of paying attention to large-scale features of a system rather than the smaller elements that make up the system. Studies suggest that with many such systems, including human consciousness, better predictions can be made by ignoring the little details and focusing on the big picture. This finding helps explain why high performers in a variety of roles, including military commanders, corporate executives, and, yes, sports coaches tend to make decisions based on limited but selectively chosen information. Thus, where workout analysis is concerned, a little bit of the right data is better than a lot of data of any kind.

The exceptions are certain cases where problems do emerge. This is the proper time for a coach to shift their focus from the forest to the trees. Consider the example of an athlete who exhibits a pattern of hitting the wall during long runs performed in humid conditions. By looking closely at the data, a coach might find that a certain dew point threshold is associated with these episodes and that a sudden spike in heart rate precedes each of them.

The coach can then use this information to prevent future bonks and gradually push back the athlete's dew-point limit by advising the athlete to quit voluntarily the moment their heart rate spikes, and also by factoring weather forecasts into planning for long runs. This example is highly particular, but it embodies broad principles for analyzing and addressing problems that occur, or are revealed, within workouts.

Measurement Bias

Measurement bias is a tendency to pay too much attention to, and to inflate the importance of, certain things just because they happen to be measured. This is a widespread problem among athletes and coaches alike. A good example is functional threshold power (FTP), which is the highest wattage an athlete can sustain for one hour on a bike. Many cyclists and triathletes use FTP tests to calculate their training zones and track changes in fitness. But FTP is just one of many different ways to measure fitness, and it has little practical relevance in certain situations. For these reasons, it is a mistake for athletes to assume that increasing their FTP is always an important priority. Consider the example of an ultra-endurance cyclist training for a multiday transcontinental race. For this athlete, improving the fat-burning capacity of the muscles is far more important than increasing FTP, and in fact, if the athlete is training correctly for such an event, their FTP should plateau or even decrease slightly in the last several weeks before the event. That's because it is almost impossible for an already-fit cyclist to increase their FTP on a training program that heavily emphasizes overall volume and prolonged individual rides at low intensity, as an ultra-endurance cycling program should do in the peak phase of training.

Athletes are prone to seek improvement in any measurable challenge you put in front of them, whether it's a lactate threshold test, a body composition test, a VO_2max test, a sit-and-reach test, a single-repetition strength test, or something else. But as with FTP, the results of these challenges are not equally important to all athletes in every situation, and pursuing improvement in any one of them at the wrong time could negatively impact fitness components that actually are important. For example, if a triathlete's anaerobic capacity (defined as the amount of work an athlete can perform at extremely high intensity) increases during the final phase of training for an Ironman triathlon, that's a bad thing, as there is no way an athlete can train appropriately for maximum performance in an Ironman, which is a 99 percent aerobic event, and also gain anaerobic fitness.

Be wary of measurement bias in monitoring and assessing your athletes' training. Consider which components of fitness they should be improving in, which ones they should be content to maintain, and which are irrelevant. Communicate this information to your athletes so they don't become distracted by irrelevant measurements and are not alarmed or frustrated by a lack of improvement in a fitness component that's low on the priority scale.

Best Practices for Measuring Performance

Within a race-focused macrocycle, athletes should be improving in at least one component of their fitness at any given time. The specific components that should see measurable improvement vary depending on where the athlete is within the macrocycle and the type of race they're training for. Generally speaking, the fitness component you should monitor most closely for improvement during a given phase of training matches the top-ranked training priority for that same phase in Tables 5.3–5.7 in the preceding chapter. It is also generally the case that athletes should experience improvement in a variety of fitness components in the base phase of training, when they are relatively far from peak fitness, and experience further improvement in fewer and fewer components as they approach peak fitness. And, of course, improvement should also be seen in any fitness component that is newly introduced to training or newly emphasized. For example, an athlete without a prior history of stretching who starts a structured mobility program is likely to see steady increases in mobility for some time.

Key workouts that are specific to a fitness component that is being emphasized in a particular phase of training are the best tests of improvement (*principle of specificity*). To serve their intended purpose, these workouts must challenge an athlete's limits in that component, for this is precisely how they increase fitness. But in challenging an athlete's limits, these workouts also measure limits, and in this way, they gauge the effectiveness of the training. The training is the testing, in this case.

Physiological performance tests that fall outside the normal course of training can be useful benchmarks of improvement, but be mindful of their limitations. For example, it goes without saying that a VO_2max test is a good way to measure improvements in an athlete's aerobic capacity, and there are certain moments within a training cycle when VO_2max should be increasing. Still, don't lose sight of the fact that no athlete trains to win VO$_2$max tests, nor are these tests as effective as actual workouts (e.g., lactate intervals) in increasing this fitness component.

The same advice applies to any and all tests that are used to determine an athlete's intensity zones. A wide range of options are available for this purpose. Some of these tests have the potential to function as relevant markers of an athlete's fitness development while also serving their main function of establishing or updating zones. For example, 20-minute time trials are often used for intensity zone calibration and recalibration. By definition, a 20-minute time trial is performed at an intensity that corresponds to critical power/velocity, so if this test happens to be done in a phase of training where CP/CV is prioritized, it has somewhat more relevance than the same test does when conducted in a phase of training where VO$_2$max is the highest priority. Don't fall into the trap of assuming every athlete should always perform better in whichever test is used to determine intensity zones.

Many of today's endurance training devices have the capability to auto-calculate fitness and performance indicators such as VO$_2$max and lactate threshold heart rate on the fly using regular workout data. While this is nice in theory, such estimates are unreliable and should be verified against more reliable data sources or ignored altogether. Just because a computer says something doesn't mean it's true.

Coaches often need to remind athletes that they must avoid placing too much emphasis on any single workout as an assessment of how the training process is going. We need to heed the same advice in reviewing objective data. If an athlete's training load is increasing, and if the athlete is generally feeling on top of (or at least equal to) their training, then it's safe to say the process is going well, even if no single workout performance is spectacular.

Subjective Reports

Subjective reports are different from objective data in two key respects, which together make this category of information easy to overlook. The first is that, whereas objective data speaks for itself, subjective reports must be solicited from athletes. The second difference is that subjective reports aren't really measurable, and as such they tend to be undervalued by coaches prone to measurement bias. Yet although subjective reports are easier than objective data to overlook, they are no less useful in keeping athletes on track, so it's essential that you establish a system for receiving regular subjective reports from your athletes. This can be done in person or through phone or online interactions.

There are three main categories of information you'll want to glean from athletes' subjective reports: emotional status, perceived challenge, and aches and pains. Let's have a closer look at each.

EMOTIONAL STATUS

Athletes make the most progress when their motivation level is high and they are having fun (*principle of enjoyment*). Low or declining levels of motivation or enjoyment are as much a problem as a failed workout and should receive a similar response from the coach. Whenever a problem of this sort comes about, try to identify the cause and then make targeted efforts to address it. Suppose an athlete you're working with experiences a dip in motivation resulting from a race cancellation. Instead of passively waiting for the athlete's motivation to return, you might come up with an alternative challenge for them to focus on.

PERCEIVED CHALLENGE

As important as knowing how athletes feel about their training emotionally is knowing how their training feels perceptually—in particular, how challenging they perceive it to be. If an athlete breezes through a workout you expected to be quite hard for them, it's safe to raise the bar in future workouts. But unless the athlete reports this information, your future prescriptions might be needlessly conservative. So be sure to solicit such feedback as a matter of routine.

Keep tabs on how challenging the training process feels to your athletes more broadly as well. Sometimes athletes feel on top of their training, other times they feel on par with their current training load, and in certain moments they might feel their training is *on top of them*. None of these states is inherently good or bad. Each is appropriate at different points of the process. In the early part of a macrocycle, the expectation is that athletes feel on top of their training, confident they could handle more. In the middle and latter parts of a macrocycle, they will likely feel on par with their training load most of the time—challenged but not overwhelmed. The exception is those brief periods of planned functional overreaching, when it's okay if they briefly feel a bit overmatched. Ultimately, the only way you will know if your athlete is appropriately challenged by their training at any given time is if you request routine subjective reports that include this level of detail.

ACHES AND PAINS

Regularly monitoring musculoskeletal discomfort in your athletes will help you help them avoid injuries. Pain is not merely unpleasant; it is valuable information. Athletes who, with the help of a coach, correctly interpret their pain experiences and respond appropriately will encounter fewer injury-induced disruptions to their training.

Recognize that pain is normal and not something that athletes should try to avoid at all costs. Nor does pain always indicate injury. It is far more often a warning of potential injury than a signal that an injury has occurred. The thing you want to avoid is allowing pain in a given area to increase over time. Mild to moderate levels of pain are typically okay to train through as long as they do not trend upward within a workout or from one workout to the next. Recognize, however, that pain can be unpredictable and is experienced differently by different athletes. Effective pain management often requires a degree of trial and error to best accommodate the athlete (*principle of individualization*).

Managing Injuries: A Case Study in Problem-Solving

Few problems are more disruptive to training than injury. For this reason, injuries offer the perfect example for illustrating how coaches should problem-solve. First off, understand that injuries are part of being an endurance athlete and are not always the result of a mistake. To train at the level that is required to achieve peak fitness, one must accept some risk of injury. An endurance athlete who has never been injured is likely an athlete who has not yet realized their full potential!

What is a mistake, however, is allowing small injuries to become big ones. By catching and reacting early to warning signs of potential injury, a coach can avoid this mistake. It's a team effort, and it's on the athlete to communicate their aches and pains to their coach *as they occur*. Unfortunately, many athletes only share this information when it's already too late. Again, pain does not equal injury, but nearly all significant injuries are heralded by pain, so the coach's role in the effort to avoid injury is to identify which pain episodes are benign and which demand a response of some kind, and then coordinate a specific response.

Note that overreacting to warning signs of a potential injury is just as problematic as underreacting. Too many athletes take an all-or-nothing approach to training, plowing through small niggles and backing off excessively in reaction to more severe pain episodes. It's better to practice a strategy of incremental retreat when threat of injury arises. This entails modifying training by the least amount required to attenuate the risk of a bigger breakdown. The specifics of what this looks like depend on the situation. Options include shortening or reducing the intensity of one or more workouts, switching to a cross-training modality that causes less or no pain, moving one or more workouts to different terrain, making equipment modifications, and introducing corrective measures such as rehabilitative exercises.

If the initial modification you try doesn't do the trick, retreat another step (*principle of adaptivity*), and if the next modification doesn't work, retreat some more, always giving up the least ground necessary. Be aware that, in some cases, retreating by the smallest increment necessary to avoid making things worse does entail resting the affected part of the body. In these cases it may be advisable for the athlete to also seek help from an orthopedist, sports medicine specialist, or physiotherapist. Such measures should be a last resort, but it is a step that many athletes have to take at some point.

As an endurance coach, you are not expected to be an expert on sports injuries. That being said, it is helpful to have some knowledge in this area, as it will enable you to determine when it is safe for an athlete to train through an issue and when more radical concessions are necessary. Experience will teach you most of what you need to know, but if you'd like to take a more proactive approach to educating yourself on this topic, check out the Resources section for more on this topic.

Regardless of how much or how little you know about sports injuries, we recommend that you develop a network of trusted professionals to whom you can refer athletes when necessary. In cases where the injured athlete is someone you work with remotely, they may have to rely on their own network for treatment, but there is a lot that can be done from a distance in terms of diagnosis and counsel. Specific types of specialists you might wish to refer athletes to for remote consultations are physiotherapists, sports medicine physicians, strength and conditioning coaches, sports nutritionists, and sports psychologists.

A REVIEW OF THE PROBLEM-SOLVING PROCESS

The foregoing discussion of injury management is intended to serve as an example of how coaches should address problems of all kinds that affect their athletes. While each specific type of problem, including injury, requires responsive measures that are unique to that problem, the process of coaching athletes through problems is universal:

1. Monitor your athletes' training daily, focusing narrowly on the most pertinent objective data and subjective reports with an eye toward identifying problems.
2. When a problem is identified, modify subsequent training in targeted ways to correct the problem or limit its impact, departing from the original script as much as necessary but no more.
3. Be willing to lean on outside resources as needed to get the athlete back on track.

Finally, resist the urge to differentiate too much between "on track" periods and "off track" periods in your athletes' training. Instead, regard the training process as one continuous push against challenges and limitations both big and small. Your role as the coach never changes. Whether your athletes are on track or off, it's your job to identify and adaptively address the problems they encounter in their training. The best coaches are neither content when problems are few and small nor frustrated when problems are large and many. To them it's all the same journey, and let it be so for you too.

Sport–Specific Considerations

⚊ At a broad level, best practices in endurance training (namely the 80/20 method) apply to all endurance sports, but at the level of specifics, somewhat different methods work best in each. We recommend that coaches concentrate on just one or two sports to better serve their athletes.

⚊ For some sports, such as off-road cycling and running, workouts and/or terrain might have to be adjusted to maintain the appropriate intensity balance.

⚊ Considerations such as injury prevention and skill building will necessarily influence how coaches approach sports like running and swimming. In all cases, the approach needs to be based on the individual needs of the athlete.

There is no universally recognized definition of an endurance sport. That's kind of surprising, because it's not hard to come up with one. In fact, let's give it a try: The goal in any race, regardless of length, is to reach the finish line in the least time possible. Achieving this goal requires very different strategies in shorter races than it does in longer races. Science has demonstrated that a truly maximal physical effort cannot be sustained longer than about 45 seconds. In races lasting less than 45 seconds, the surest way to reach the finish line in the least time possible is to go as fast as possible the whole way through. In longer races, this is not the case. To complete these races in the least time possible, athletes must consciously hold back, working at submaximal intensity until they are within about 45 seconds of the finish line. Longer races must be paced, in other words. An endurance sport, then, is any sport in which races are long enough that they must be paced.

A long list of sports fit this definition, from distance running to stand-up paddleboarding. One might reasonably expect similar training methods to yield optimal performance across the full range of endurance disciplines thus defined, and as we've seen, elite best practices confirm this expectation. In Chapter 3, we noted that elite endurance athletes in a variety of disciplines attain similar peak training loads through a combination of high volume and an 80/20 intensity balance, which indicates that superficial differences in the ways elite athletes in the various endurance sports prepare for competition are just that—superficial. Additional evidence, gathered from observational studies of elite athletes as well as from controlled studies involving recreational athletes, reinforces the idea that a high-volume, mostly low-intensity training approach is required to maximize endurance fitness and performance in all endurance sports and at every level of athletic ability and experience.

We mustn't overstate the sameness of the many endurance disciplines, however. If these sports were family members, they would be first cousins, not twins. For example, rowing requires greater strength than running, while swimming is vastly more technique-intensive than cycling. This is why specific training practices differ at the elite level between endurance disciplines. Elite rowers invest more time and energy in developing their strength than elite runners do, elite swimmers pay more attention to technique than elite cyclists do, and so on. Though superficial, such differences are important.

There's a reason we don't see many successful cross-country ski coaches who also train mountain bikers, or many well-regarded obstacle race coaches who coach aquathlon racers as well. The fact that the 80/20 Endurance training method applies to all endurance sports doesn't mean it's a good idea for you or anyone else to coach athletes in all endurance sports. As the saying goes, "A jack of all trades is a master of none." If you want to do a lot of good for a lot of athletes, don't spread yourself too thin. Instead, get to know one or two sports really well and train athletes in those one or two sports exclusively.

If the previous chapter was all about the principle of adaptivity, this one is all about the *principle of specificity*. It has two main objectives. First, it underscores the importance of tailoring the 80/20 Endurance methodology to the specific demands of each individual sport. The following survey of major endurance sports will reveal clear patterns that collectively function as a general blueprint for applying the 80/20 method to individual sports. Recognizing these patterns may help you coach the sport or sports in which you specialize more effectively while enabling you to broaden your coaching repertoire if you so choose. At the most basic level, applying the 80/20 approach to specific sports is a matter of adapting universal principles and established best practices to the special demands that make each sport unique. The brisk tour of endurance disciplines you're about to embark on will highlight the special demands of each and identify proven practices for meeting those demands.

The second goal of this chapter is to help you become a better endurance coach by widening your perspective. Similar to how traveling to a foreign country can, through contrast, teach you things about your own country, learning about less-familiar endurance sports can teach you lessons that are applicable to the sport or sports you coach. An important difference between the 80/20 system and other endurance training systems is that it is not specific to a single sport but encompasses the full range of endurance sports. Even though few coaches train athletes effectively in more than one or two disciplines, those with an "80/20 mindset" will pay more attention to sports outside their expertise, appreciating their relevance. More than once in the modern history of endurance sports, innovations in one discipline have crossed over to others in beneficial ways. Whether or not you care to be remembered for revolutionizing your sport, taking an interest in a variety of endurance sports will enrich your overall learning and supply you with ideas that have the potential to benefit your athletes.

Cycling

A plurality of endurance-related scientific studies use cyclists as their subjects, or else use indoor cycling as their experimental exercise modality. That's because cycling is a simple and highly controllable form of exercise, hence amenable to use in formal testing. For the same reasons, training for cycling events is comparatively simple and straightforward. Elite cyclists typically ride once a day, six to seven days a week, with two to three harder sessions spaced across the week. This simple formula can be adapted to meet the needs of virtually any cyclist.

Having said this, we hasten to add that there is plenty of nuance involved in perfecting the training of each individual cyclist. Training methods continue to evolve, and if you coach cyclists, you'll want to keep pace with this evolution lest you fall behind other coaches who do. Depletion rides, which entail riding in a glycogen-depleted state; variable-intensity interval rides, where cyclists toggle between an intensity close to VO_2max and an intensity closer to functional threshold power as a way to boost total session time at or near maximal oxygen update; and block periodization, which was discussed in Chapter 5, are just a few examples of methods widely used at the elite level today that were not widely used a generation ago.

The key difference between cycling and most other endurance sports is the role of technology. Performance in bike races depends not just on the body and mind of the athlete but also, to a significant degree, on the bike, components, wheels, and tires used, as well as on such details as rider positioning and tire pressure. To be an effective cycling coach, you must either know a lot about bikes, collaborate with someone (such as an expert bike fitter) who does, or limit yourself to coaching riders who themselves know a lot about bikes or have access to professionals who do. The last thing you want to do as a cycling coach is allow your athletes to lose to less-fit competitors because of a techno-logical disadvantage.

The cycling subdisciplines of mountain biking and gravel racing are different enough from road cycling as to legitimately qualify as distinct sports. Both place a premium on technical skills, such that not every great road racer can become a great off-road racer. Optimizing training for off-road competition requires a careful balancing of trail riding with rides done on the road and indoors. The obvious benefit of trail riding is that it develops the technical skills that are essential to success in mountain biking and gravel racing. The disadvantage of trail riding is that it's difficult to perform structured workouts off-road and difficult as well to stay at low intensity.

The specific balance of trail vs. non-trail riding that a given athlete does should be decided on the basis of three factors: access, preference, and skill. Athletes for whom regular trail access poses a challenge should make an effort to train off-road at least once a week. Otherwise, they will lack sufficient technical preparation for racing. Athletes who strongly prefer riding on trails should be encouraged to suck it up and ride on the road or indoors a few times each week. This is necessary to ensure they are able to maintain an 80/20 intensity balance and perform structured workouts that are difficult to do on trails. Highly skilled mountain bikers and gravel racers can get away with training off-road less often than riders at lower levels of expertise. The latter should hit the trails a few times a week, while a master bike handler may be able to maintain their skills with as little as one trail ride per week.

The fittest athletes can complete trail rides entirely at low intensity provided the terrain isn't too hilly or technical. For all others, the impossibility of staying at low intensity in these environments should be factored into planning. This can be done by determining how much time a given athlete actually spends at various intensities on a given route. For example, suppose a 3-hour endurance ride that an athlete would do entirely in Zone 2 on the road turns out to include 80 minutes of work in Zone X or above when done on a particular trail route. To make space for this session in the athlete's schedule going forward, simply subtract 80 minutes of work at Zone X and above from the rest of the week in the planning process.

Running

With the possible exception of wrestling, running is the oldest and most primitive of all sports. That doesn't mean it's easy to coach runners successfully, however, and in fact it's not. Running differs from other endurance sports in one crucial respect, which is its high-impact nature. Simply stated, running is hard on the body, the injury rate among runners vastly exceeding the injury rates in cycling, swimming, and other nonimpact endurance sports. For running coaches, the goal of keeping athletes healthy stands alongside that of building fitness as the top priority in planning, monitoring, and managing the training process.

In nonimpact endurance disciplines, athletes are generally able to absorb the volume of training that is required to maximize their fitness without undue risk of injury. In running, this is seldom the case, except at the elite level, where athletes are blessed with the low body weight and biomechanical efficiency needed to stay healthy despite heavy training loads. This isn't to say that runners who lack these blessings must resign themselves to peaking at training loads well below their theoretical limit, leaving a sizeable portion of their fitness potential untapped. By supplementing a manageable volume of running with nonimpact cross-training, even the most injury-prone runner can have it both ways, avoiding frequent injury without lowering their performance and fitness standards.

Some runners are resistant to cross-training because either they aren't wholly convinced of its effectiveness or they don't enjoy it as much as they do running, or both. You can help athletes overcome their skepticism about cross-training by sharing some of the abundant research proving that supplemental cross-training elevates fitness in runners (check out the Resources at the back of the book for one example) and by offering real-world examples of runners who have achieved success through cross-training. At the same time, you can make cross-training more palatable to runners who don't enjoy it by encouraging them to choose the specific modality they find most palatable (*principle of enjoyment*). The most beneficial cross-training activities for runners are those that, like running, involve cyclical movement of the legs. Options include indoor and outdoor cycling, elliptical running, outdoor elliptical biking, incline treadmill walking, antigravity treadmill running, pool running, slideboarding, and cross-country skiing. Runners should feel free to pick their favorite from this list or use more than one activity if variety enhances their enjoyment of cross-training.

The specific balance of running and cross-training that co-optimizes fitness development and injury prevention differs from one runner to the next. Three runs per week is the minimum for improvement in running. Twelve to thirteen total sessions per week (running and cross-training combined) will suffice to maximize fitness in those runners who have the time, the motivation, and the physical capacity to train this often. Hence, a runner who is strongly prone to injury but is willing and able to maintain a high frequency of aerobic training is likely to get the best results from running three times per week and cross-training nine or ten times. But for another runner—older or younger, more experienced or less, faster or slower—the optimal balance might be six runs per week and two cross-training sessions, or four runs per week and one cross-training session, or even thirteen runs per week and zero cross-training, just like the pros.

You'll probably need to experiment a bit to find the right balance of running and cross-training for each runner (*principle of individualization*), and that balance might change over time. Use the following two-tier hierarchy of priorities to guide this process:

1. **Find out how much running the athlete can handle before their injury risk becomes unacceptable.** As effective as cross-training is for runners, nothing beats running as a stimulus for running performance.

2. **Find the combined running/cross-training load that maximizes the athlete's running performance.** In other words, find a training load sweet spot for the athlete that includes both their running and their supplemental aerobic training, just as you would with a triathlete or other multisport athlete. If a runner's running tolerance is lower than their overall endurance training tolerance, some amount of supplemental cross-training is merited.

As in cycling, running has subdisciplines that require specific preparation. All of the guidelines for balancing off-road training with road and indoor training supplied in the preceding section in reference to mountain bikers and gravel racers apply to trail runners as well. If the athlete races mostly or entirely on trails, they should train off-road once a week at least and a few times at most, choosing controlled environments (road, track, treadmill) for structured workouts and flatter, nontechnical venues for runs intended to be done entirely at low intensity.

Swimming

On a competitive level, the most notable difference between the sport of swimming and other endurance sports is the brevity of races. The longest Olympic swimming event (besides the 10 km open-water event) is the 1500-meter freestyle, which on a time basis is roughly the equivalent of the 5 km distance in running and the 15-km time-trial distance in road cycling. Yet despite how short pool swimming competitions are, elite swimmers train at equally high volume as elite athletes in other endurance sports and also do 80 percent of their swimming at low intensity.

There are two reasons for this. First, with the exception of sprint specialists, swimmers need to maximize their aerobic capacity and endurance to be successful at the highest level, and as we know, high volume and an approximate 80/20 intensity balance are required to maximize aerobic capacity and endurance. Second, swimming performance depends to a significant degree on efficiency in the water, and efficiency in the water improves with time in the water, almost without limit.

In essence, then, the fact that swimming races are generally shorter than races in other endurance sports makes no practical difference in terms of how swimmers train. But there's another difference between swimming and its endurance cousins that does affect training, and that, of course, is the importance of technique to swimming performance. To maximize speed and efficiency in the water, swimmers must devote a lot of time to working on technique. As noted, time in the water is an effective way of improving efficiency. A swimmer who trains with a strict focus on fitness and never thinks about their technique will become more efficient for this reason. However, it is impossible to fully optimize one's technique in this manner.

Optimal freestyle swim technique is simply too complex and nuanced for individual swimmers to figure out for themselves through independent trial-and-error. To maximize their rate of improvement in this skill, swimmers must undergo a comprehensive learning process guided by an expert coach. This process has six key elements: stroke analysis, instruction/demonstration, proprioceptive cues, swim aids, technique drills, and strength and mobility work. Let's briefly review the role of each.

Stroke Analysis

Inexpert swimmers are not all inexpert for the same reason. Some need work on their body position, others need work on their rotation, still others need work on their stroke finish, and so on. The appropriate starting point of the technique improvement process, therefore, is a visual analysis of the individual swimmer's current stroke that serves the purpose of identifying specific areas that need work (*principle of individualization*). This can be done either with the naked eye or by video, but video is superior because it allows the coach to study the stroke at reduced speed and to freeze the stroke at various points. The analysis itself consists of cataloging things the swimmer is doing right as well as imperfections that need to be addressed.

Most swimmers have multiple stroke imperfections. With these athletes, it is not possible to address all of the things that need work simultaneously. Throwing too many corrections at a swimmer at one time is likely to overwhelm them, causing frustration and slowing improvement. It's better to create a hierarchy of imperfections and address no more than two or three together, starting with those that are judged to have the greatest negative impact on the swimmer's speed and efficiency. When sufficient improvement has occurred in these areas, new points of emphasis can be introduced. Note that because all parts of the freestyle swim stroke are interconnected, fixing one imperfection sometimes has a positive ripple effect on others. For example, correcting under-rotation may improve a swimmer's breathing efficiency.

Visual analysis should be performed not once but regularly. With inexperienced and less proficient swimmers it can be done as frequently as every other week or so. With more experienced and proficient swimmers, video analysis can be done as an occasional audit of the stroke to ensure former bad habits don't creep back in.

Instruction/Demonstration

Having identified the imperfections in a swimmer's stroke, the coach must then communicate the necessary improvements through instruction and demonstration. First, the coach must explain the difference between correct and incorrect technique in a particular part of the stroke. Although verbal communication has little power in itself to effect technique improvements, it is an essential part of the process because it gives the swimmer a high-level conceptual understanding of what they are trying to achieve in the water. Words like "tautness" and "relaxed" are used to describe an aspect of swim technique with good success.

Naturally, the next step is for the coach to visually demonstrate examples of correct and incorrect technique for the swimmer. These can take a variety of forms, including live demonstrations on dry land or in the water, "mirroring" exercises, or videos of other swimmers executing correct or incorrect form.

As with stroke analysis, a lot of repetition is required to get the most out of instruction and demonstration. The aim of swim technique coaching is to rewire the brain's motor program for swimming, which is not a "one-and-done" affair. Coaches must be prepared to frequently reinforce the same messaging in the instruction/demonstration component of teaching swim technique.

Proprioceptive Cues

Proprioceptive cues are images, kinesthetic prompts, and other mental tools that help swimmers execute technique elements correctly. A familiar example is "press the buoy," a cue that instructs swimmers to imagine pressing a small buoy down into the water with their chest as a way to correct the common error of swimming "uphill" (i.e., with the hips and legs well below the waterline).

Scores of different proprioceptive cues have been employed over the years, with varying degrees of success. Individual coaches tend to have their own personal favorites, but every coach should be open to trying different ones with each swimmer, as cues that don't work for some swimmers do work for others. What's most important is that the coach make regular use of proprioceptive cues of some kind in teaching swimming technique. After all, a swimmer has to think about *something* while swimming, and well-chosen proprioceptive cues keep their mind focused on simple, relevant guides to correct movement. In this way, such cues are more helpful than any other thoughts a swimmer might entertain in the water.

Swim Aids

Equipment such as hand paddles, fins, snorkels, pull buoys, and tempo trainers help swimmers learn better technique. The advantage of swim aids is that they all but force the swimmer to swim with better technique, so they don't have to think about what they're doing as much. The essence of mastery in any motor skill is the ability to do it almost unconsciously, with minimal mental effort. Whereas proprioceptive cues improve technique from the inside out (from thought to action), swim aids do so from the outside in, allowing the mind to get used to the feeling of moving correctly in a passive, receptive manner.

The risk with swim aids is that, like many tools, they can become crutches if relied on too heavily. The best swim coaches integrate the use of swim aids into training in a judicious way that keeps them from becoming crutches. An example is having an athlete swim with an ankle band in the first 50-meter lap in a set of 200-meter intervals to get them used to the feeling of swimming with a tighter kick and then trying to maintain a tight kick unassisted for the remaining 150 meters.

As with proprioceptive cues, individual coaches tend to have varying opinions on which swim aids are helpful and which are useless or even counterproductive. Form your own opinions through experience rather than assume any single coach is right about everything.

But among the most successful swim coaches there is a general consensus that thoughtful use of swim aids yields better results than eschewing them altogether.

Technique Drills

Technique drills are modified versions of swimming that are intended to stimulate improvement in a specific technique element—for example, swimming with fisted hands to enforce a high-elbow catch. There is a great deal of debate among coaches concerning just how useful drills are in developing better freestyle swim technique. Unfortunately, little scientific evidence exists to settle this debate one way or the other. It's likely, however, that the answer varies from one drill to the next and also, to some extent, from one swimmer to the next. The surest bets are drills that, like the fist drill, all but force the athlete to move correctly and that translate directly to normal swimming. (The fist drill *is* normal swimming, except with closed hands.)

Scores of different drills have been created over the decades. We advise swim coaches to learn and test as many as seem worth testing. Through this process you will amass a collection of favorites and learn which individual drills are most effective in helping athletes overcome specific technique imperfections. There should be no stopping point in this process, no matter how long you've been coaching. If you continuously discover new and different drills and revisit old or forgotten ones, you will keep finding ways to improve your overall repertoire.

Strength and Mobility Work

Some swim stroke imperfections are not the result of technique errors per se, but are instead a consequence of limitations in strength and mobility. Certain technique fixes can be difficult or impossible for a swimmer to execute unless they become stronger or more mobile, thereby enabling their body to move in the desired way. Unlike other methods of swim technique instruction, this one does have scientific support, if only because it's easier to test—a number of studies have shown beneficial effects of "dryland" training on swimming performance. We will have more to say on this topic in Chapter 8.

————

It goes without saying that, in order to coach swimmers effectively, you must either be or become an expert in technique. Such expertise is not strictly necessary for coaches who work remotely with triathlon swimmers only, though it is certainly useful. If you do work with triathletes, or you wish to, you will at least want to have a professional relationship with an expert in freestyle swim technique so you can refer athletes for video analysis and feedback. If you wish to pursue your own mastery of swim technique instruction, make use of the Resources section at the back of the book.

Triathlon

In triathlon and other multidisciplinary endurance sports, the *principle of balance* takes on new importance, functioning on two distinct levels. Like other endurance athletes, multisport athletes need to balance their training intensities optimally. That's level one. But at the same time, these athletes must also balance their training in the distinct disciplines that make up their sport, something that single-discipline endurance athletes don't have to worry about.

As a relatively new sport originating in the late 1970s, triathlon offers a well-documented history of its training evolution. The first generation of elite triathletes engaged in a sometimes reckless game of one-upmanship in which each athlete tried to out-train the rest. The consequences for some were severe, but the process did at least serve the purpose of revealing how much was too much and how best to balance training in the water, on the bike, and on foot.

In terms of frequency, it's best to plan an equal or almost equal number of sessions in each discipline within a microcycle. In terms of time, training proportions should roughly match race proportions, where (in a short-course event) the typical athlete spends about 50 percent of their total race time on the bike and 25 percent each swimming and running. The rationale for training with equal frequency across disciplines is that it allows athletes to get stronger in their weakest discipline while maintaining strength in their strongest discipline. The rationale for distributing training time across disciplines in a way that matches race proportions is that it allows athletes to shave off the most minutes in the discipline in which there are the most minutes to be shaved (cycling).

Many triathletes make the mistake of overemphasizing their strongest discipline, which is almost always also the discipline they most enjoy. Some triathlon coaches, meanwhile, make the mistake of having athletes focus too much on their weakest discipline, which, while it does tend to yield significant improvement in that discipline, often comes at the cost of fitness losses in their strongest discipline.

There is a proper time to focus on an athlete's weakest sport, but that time is generally not within a race-focused macrocycle. Swim-focused, bike-focused, and run-focused training blocks should instead be scheduled for the off-season or at other times when a race is not imminent. It's okay to place a modest emphasis on a single discipline within the training cycle, but the key word here is *modest*. Examples are adding once-weekly swim technique lessons to an athlete's schedule to address weakness in this discipline, scheduling back-to-back long rides on some weekends to accelerate improvement in cycling, and having an athlete complete a short transition run after every bike session for a period of time to help their running catch up to their swimming and cycling.

As for swim-focused, bike-focused, and run-focused training blocks done outside a triathlete's primary training cycle culminating in multisport events, it is recommended that these culminate with a race in *that* discipline. After all, this is precisely how swimmers get better at swimming, cyclists get better at cycling, and runners get better at running—not by training to train but by training to race. You might, for example, train a triathlete with a weak swim for an open-water swim event, train a triathlete who's less proficient on the bike for a Gran Fondo, or train a triathlete with a slower run for a half marathon. In each of these scenarios, training frequency in the athlete's weak discipline should increase while frequency in the other two disciplines is reduced, though not all the way to zero, as this would put them in a hole that would be difficult to climb out of when they returned to normal triathlon training.

On this last point, it's okay and even expected for athletes to lose some fitness in the disciplines they are placing on the metaphorical backburner during these single-sport focus periods. Some athletes balk at this, but the lost fitness will come back quickly, and athletes seldom regret the commitment they make to shoring up a weakness.

These same general principles apply to other multisport events such as aquathlon, duathlon, and winter triathlon. Only the specifics differ. Similarly, the guidelines for off-road cycling, open-water swimming, and trail running presented in earlier sections apply to off-road triathlon training.

Obstacle Course Racing

The thing that makes obstacle course racing (OCR) different from other endurance sports—and from running in particular—couldn't be more obvious: the obstacles that participants must negotiate along the course. Remove these elements and OCR becomes a typical cross country running event. That being said, the type of fitness that is required to negotiate obstacle challenges such as wall climbs is very different from the type of fitness involved in endurance running. This is why training for OCR is so different from training for cross country running.

Obstacle elements demand a mix of strength, muscular endurance, agility, and specific skill in each individual obstacle type. The best way to train for this component of OCR is through a combination of functional strength training (covered in Chapter 8), high-intensity calisthenics such as burpees and pull-ups, and actual obstacle practice, if possible. All endurance athletes should incorporate functional strength work into their training, but because strength makes a bigger contribution to OCR performance, this type of training should receive greater emphasis in OCR training. We recommend that OCR athletes complete two to three sessions per week of functional strength training and high-intensity calisthenics combined. Functional strength should receive greater emphasis in the early part of the macrocycle, while in the last several weeks before a race the emphasis should shift to high-intensity calisthenics. Examples of how both types of workouts should be structured can be found at 8020endurance.com.

Specific obstacle skills training is highly beneficial to OCR performance but it can be rather impractical. Not many of us have monster truck tires lying around our backyards! To the extent that athletes do have access to obstacle equipment, they should try to complete a few practice sessions with them before each race. If you specialize or wish to specialize in coaching OCR athletes, it is advisable that you either create or link up with a facility that has such equipment.

As important as the obstacle-related components of fitness are to OCR performance, running fitness is more important and is therefore not to be overlooked. All of the 80/20 endurance training principles and methods that apply to other running disciplines apply here as well. Just a few adaptations need to be made for the specific demands of OCR. These are as follows:

⌐ High-intensity calisthenics workouts and obstacle skills training sessions performed at a high tempo qualify as high-intensity endurance training sessions, and as such they affect the amount of moderate- and high-intensity running athletes can and should do. When planning microcycles, make sure that the athlete spends no more than 20 percent of their training time at these intensities, whether in runs or other workouts.

⌁ Some training runs should be punctuated with short bouts of calisthenics exercises and/or obstacle negotiation to provide specific practice for events.

⌁ Similarly, some training runs should be performed on technical trails similar to those that are common in obstacle course races.

GOING DEEPER

Because this book is concerned with teaching principles and methods that apply broadly to all endurance sports, it cannot teach the technical aspects of any single sport in detail. If you wish to deepen your technical knowledge of a particular sport (and we suggest you do), start with the Resources at the back of the book. Among the sport-specific sources of technical learning you will find there are some that deal with sports not discussed in this chapter, such as rowing and ski mountaineering.

Strength and Mobility Training

⟋ Like the endurance training plans coaches create for their athletes, strength and mobility programs should be modeled after elite best practices.

⟋ Even small amounts of strength and mobility training are highly beneficial. Don't hesitate to provide time-efficient programs for athletes who are resistant to strength and mobility training.

⟋ Avoid prescribing one-size-fits-all strength and mobility programs. Instead, individualize them by athlete type, experience level, physical limiters, etc.

Today's top endurance athletes do not limit their training to the activity or activities they compete in. Elite swimmers do more than swim, professional cyclists do more than ride their bikes, and world-class runners do more than run. All of these athletes supplement their endurance training with strength workouts and mobility exercises. While it is difficult to make the case that these ancillary training modalities are essential to competitive success, those whose livelihood depends on their performance do them for a reason. Both real-world and scientific evidence suggest that strength and mobility training reduce injury risk, enhance performance, and dampen the negative effects of aging on fitness and performance. It is fair to say, then, that every serious endurance athlete ought to train routinely for strength and mobility—which means every endurance coach should have a system for ensuring their athletes are set up with effective strength and mobility programs.

One option is to develop sufficient expertise in strength and mobility training so you can create high-quality strength and mobility programs for athletes. The other option is to delegate this service to a specialist in these areas. At the elite level, most endurance coaches delegate. Professional endurance athletes require strength and mobility programs that are every bit as sophisticated as their endurance training programs. It can be difficult for any individual coach to attain equal levels of expertise in endurance, strength, and mobility training. On the other hand, the average endurance coach can become knowledgeable enough about strength and mobility training to create programs that are efficient and effective for their athletes.

It is beyond the scope of this chapter to provide a complete education in endurance-focused strength and mobility coaching, but it will provide a solid conceptual foundation for meeting the strength and mobility needs of your athletes. To do this, you will need to know how to acquire relevant knowledge of strength and mobility training, how to schedule strength workouts and mobility sessions, and how to tailor ancillary training programs to athletes in different sports and to individual needs.

Gaining Knowledge

If your goal was to get a job as the head strength coach for a professional cycling team, and to become as knowledgeable as possible about ancillary training methods for endurance sports, your best move would be to pursue a recognized gold-standard credential in strength and conditioning. In North America, the National Strength and Conditioning Association's Certified Strength and Conditioning Specialist (CSCS) credential carries the most clout. To earn it, you must first obtain a college degree (the specific subject doesn't matter) and then you must pay a registration fee, study, and pass a four-hour exam that covers exercise science, sport psychology, nutrition, exercise technique, program design, organization and administration, and testing and evaluation. But if you don't care about the credential and are interested only in the underlying knowledge, you can obtain this by purchasing and reading the official textbooks of the CSCS program, *Exercise Technique Manual for Resistance Training* and *Essentials of Strength Training and Conditioning*.

Most experts would agree that the best way to gain bona fide expertise in strength and mobility training for endurance athletes is practical learning. Regardless of whether you choose to pursue a credential or study textbooks, the only essential requirements for coaching them competently are 1) direct interaction with experienced and successful strength and mobility coaches who can mentor you in some fashion and 2) hands-on practice, preferably under the initial guidance of a mentor. Coaching strength and mobility is more like woodworking than it is like particle physics in the sense that an hour of apprenticeship is worth ten hours of study. For this reason, you might want to network with one or more qualified strength and mobility coaches for a time even if you intend to handle your own strength and mobility programming eventually. By shadowing these professionals as they work with your athletes you will be more prepared to assume the additional responsibility down the road.

The field of strength and mobility training is ever-evolving; learning enough to master current practices does not guarantee you'll remain current. To avoid falling behind, set aside some time each week to peruse the relevant scientific journals and absorb the blogs, videos, and other content put out by the best and brightest up-and-coming strength and mobility coaches. A couple of examples of the latter are offered in the Resources section.

Strength Training Modalities

Before we tackle mobility, let's first describe the elite approach to strength training. The term "strength training" encompasses a variety of different methods and modalities. These include bodyweight exercises, weightlifting, Pilates, yoga, and branded methods such as

CrossFit. Recreational endurance athletes practice all of these methods, and more, with peer influence rather than expert guidance being the main driver of individual choices. The problem with this is that not all strength training activities are equally beneficial for endurance athletes, and some are even counterproductive.

For example, CrossFit is a poor choice for endurance athletes because many of the exercises included in a typical CrossFit workout are irrelevant to a majority of endurance sports. Furthermore, these workouts function more as high-intensity interval sessions than as focused strength workouts, taking away from athletes' ability to perform high-intensity interval workouts in their main sport activity or activities. CrossFit workouts also fail to include certain types of exercises that have a high degree of functional carryover to specific endurance disciplines, such as those that strengthen smaller muscles that play an important stabilizing role in particular sports movements.

In your effort to steer your athletes toward an approach to strength training that gives them the most benefit, it's helpful, once again, to look to the elites. Nearly 100 percent of elite endurance athletes practice a method of strength training that is loosely termed *functional strength training*, encompassing weightlifting, bodyweight exercises, and other strength movements involving equipment such as stability balls and resistance bands. This approach to strength training came about the same way every other universal best practice in elite endurance training came about: collective trial and error. Elite best practices in strength training for endurance sports will undoubtedly continue to be refined in the future, but recreational endurance athletes who want to benefit from the time and energy they invest in strength training will be well served to emulate the approach used by the pros.

To be clear, most types of strength training are better than omitting strength training entirely. For some endurance athletes, it truly is "yoga or nothing" or "the beach-muscle workout I've been doing since college or nothing." As an endurance coach, you might not be able to sell the elite way of training for strength to every athlete. But you should at least try.

For every endurance athlete who strength trains with suboptimal methods, there is at least one who strength trains erratically or not at all. These athletes often feel they are too busy for strength training, or they just don't like it. Your ace in the hole in working with such athletes is the fact that small amounts of strength training confer meaningful benefits.

Emulating the elite approach to strength training doesn't necessarily mean spending as much time on it as the pros do. In the same way that many recreational endurance athletes thrive best on a scaled-down version of elite endurance training, many can also gain the lion's share of the benefits of strength training through a minimalist approach to this type of training, which we will describe later in the chapter.

The same is true of mobility training. Athletes who want to get the most benefit from the time and energy they invest in mobility training should emulate the approach taken by the pros instead of using an approach that was not developed heuristically by endurance athletes. A scaled-down version of this approach confers most of the potential benefits.

Best Practices in Strength Training for Endurance Sports

Similar to endurance training, a good strength program is made up of different types of exercise and workout structures that change up load, frequency, and volume. The same *principles of progression and periodization*, *sport specificity*, and *individualization* apply to how a strength program is put together. Established best practices exist for each of these elements. Let's have a look at them.

Exercise Types

There are five different types of strength exercises that are complementary to endurance training: balance and proprioceptive exercises, corrective exercises, explosive movements, functional strength exercises, heavy lifts, and isometric exercises. Video demonstrations of the exercises in bold can be accessed in the 80/20 Endurance Strength Library.

BALANCE AND PROPRIOCEPTIVE EXERCISES

Proprioceptive exercises challenge the athlete's ability to maintain stability while moving. Balance exercises are a subtype of this type of exercise. An example is the **single-leg reverse deadlift** (or single-leg RDL). Such exercises improve balance and strengthen smaller muscles that play an important stabilizing role during sports movements, improving efficiency. This type of exercise should be done regularly in all phases of training. Balance and proprioceptive movements are especially useful in athletic pain management and in the rehabilitation of injuries, as they tend to be doable even when an athlete's functional capacity is limited in a particular area due to pain or injury.

CORRECTIVE EXERCISES

Similar to balance and proprioceptive exercises, ***corrective exercises*** strengthen smaller muscles responsible for stabilizing joints during sports movements. An example is the **band pull-apart**, which strengthens the muscles around the scapula and is helpful to swimmers, rowers, cross-country skiers, and other athletes whose sport involves cyclical movements of the arms against resistance. Corrective exercises should also be done regularly in all phases of training. Not every strength training expert loves the term *corrective exercise*, which derives from the proven usefulness of these movements in managing pain and rehabilitating injuries, but the fact of the matter is that exercises of this type are useful in managing pain and rehabilitating injuries.

EXPLOSIVE MOVEMENTS

Also known as ballistic exercises, ***explosive movements*** are strength exercises performed at high speed. An example of an explosive movement is the **kettlebell swing**. Explosive movements should be emphasized close (but not too close) to competition, especially by athletes specializing in shorter, faster events. These exercises are highly stressful to the neuromuscular system, and it doesn't take a lot of this type of training to achieve the desired effects, so there's no reason to emphasize it year-round. When races are not imminent, explosive movements should be done at a maintenance level, sufficient to ensure a smooth transition to the peak phase of training, when these movements are prioritized. Runners should privilege plyometrics or jumping exercises over other explosive exercises, as jumping movements have the greatest functional carryover to running.

FUNCTIONAL STRENGTH EXERCISES

Functional strength exercises simulate, and strengthen the body for, sport-specific actions. An example is the *reverse lunge*, which simulates sport-specific movements in cross-country skiing, running, cycling, and other sports involving cyclical leg action. These exercises can be done throughout every phase of training because they are not as stressful to the body.

HEAVY LIFTS

Heavy lifts are strength exercises involving multiple muscle groups and movement against high levels of resistance. A long list of familiar exercises fall within this category, including

barbell deadlifts and **barbell back squats**. They benefit athletes by improving the strength of large muscles that act as prime movers in the performance of sport-specific movements. Heavy lifts should be done in most phases of training, receiving the greatest emphasis when races are not imminent and less emphasis close to competition.

ISOMETRIC EXERCISES

Isometric exercises involve static muscle contractions that keep the muscle under tension for a specific period of time. An example is the **wall squat**. Isometric exercises are useful in developing muscular endurance in stabilizing muscles and during the early phases of pain management and injury rehabilitation, when the affected part of the body is not yet ready for dynamic strength movements.

Workout Structure

Elite endurance athletes seldom perform strength workouts that focus on select areas of the body (e.g., chest and shoulders), as is common among bodybuilders. Instead they prefer full-body workouts. Fortunately, it's feasible to cover everything in a single, full-body session lasting an hour or so. This allows endurance athletes to limit the frequency of strength training, which minimizes its impact on endurance workouts.

There is more than one effective way to sequence strength exercises within a workout. Grouping exercises in pairs or threes, where each exercise challenges a different set of muscles, saves time by allowing the athlete to rest one set of muscles while using others. For example, a single-leg reverse deadlift, which works the legs and buttocks, might be paired with a side plank, which works the trunk, with the athlete alternating between these two movements until the total number of prescribed sets has been completed.

The same principle can be extended to create a circuit strength workout, where one set of every exercise is completed before the athlete goes back to the beginning to do a second set, and perhaps a third. At the other end of the sequencing spectrum is the more traditional block format, where all sets of each exercise are completed before the athlete moves on to the next. This format is often favored in workouts featuring heavy lifts, which require a minute or two of whole-body rest between sets, rendering the time-saving method of exercise pairing inapplicable.

The specific combination of exercises included in full-body strength workouts should be determined by a few factors. As a general rule, full-body strength workouts should be well-rounded, featuring a combination of heavy lifts, explosive movements, and balance and proprioceptive movements. The exercises need to target both prime movers and stabilizing muscles in the legs, core, and upper body, with more time dedicated to working the muscles relied on most heavily in the athlete's primary sport activity or activities. Note that elite endurance athletes typically perform short corrective exercise sessions almost daily, eliminating the need to include these exercises in their gym sessions. Athletes who choose not to do separate corrective exercise sessions will need to make room for these exercises in their gym workouts. Another key consideration in exercise selection is where the athlete is in their training, a matter we'll address later in the chapter.

Example of a Full-Body Strength Workout for a Triathlete

In this workout exercises are meant to be performed as supersets, meaning the athlete alternates between the paired exercises until the prescribed number of sets has been completed. Then the athlete moves on to the next superset. In terms of load, "10RM" means the exercise is to be performed with a weight the athlete could lift 10 times, while "10% BW" means the exercise requires a load equal to 10 percent of the athlete's body weight.

SETS	EXERCISE	REPS / LOAD
3	Elevated Deadlift	8 reps, 10RM
2	Pallof Press	5 × 10 seconds
3	Split Squat with Counterweight	10 reps each way, 12RM
3	Single-Leg Hamstring Bridge	12 reps each leg, 10% BW
3	Kettlebell Pull-Through	45 seconds, 10% BW
3	Posterior Tibialis Heel Raise	8 reps each leg, 10RM
3	Hip Flexor Leg Swing	8 reps each leg
3	Single-Leg Band Passover	10 reps each leg, 10% BW
3	Single-Leg Row	15 reps each leg

The preceding sidebar shows an example of a full-body strength session for a triathlete. It illustrates an appropriate general workout structure in terms of the number and combination of exercises, as well as loads, sets, and repetitions. While the general format of the workout functions as a useful template for strength workout design, the specifics are not appropriate to all athletes in all situations. Links to video demonstrations of the individual exercises are available at 8020endurance.com.

Load

In the strength training context, *load* refers to how much weight or resistance is used for a given exercise and for how long. The main factors to consider in load selection are the type

LOAD GUIDELINES FOR EACH EXERCISE TYPE

HEAVY LIFTS require the greatest loads, hence the fewest repetitions per set—typically between 4 and 10 repetitions with a weight that the athlete could lift a maximum of 5 to 12 times.

EXPLOSIVE MOVEMENTS are most effective when done in sets that terminate just before the athlete begins to slow down or lose form.

Appropriate loads for **BALANCE AND PROPRIOCEPTIVE MOVEMENTS** are highly individual, but most of these movements require either a larger number of repetitions or a lengthy time quota to produce the appropriate level of fatigue. An example is the single-leg kettlebell pass over, which entails standing on one foot and passing a kettlebell back and forth from one hand to the other. Thirty seconds is a general target for this particular exercise, but a beginner might need to start at 20 seconds while an experienced athlete might find 30 seconds too easy unless they use a heavier load or are required to balance on an unstable surface.

The sweet spot for **FUNCTIONAL STRENGTH MOVEMENTS** is 8 to 12 repetitions with a load the athlete could lift 10 to 15 times.

ISOMETRIC EXERCISES are always done for time, with appropriate set duration varying widely depending on the difficulty of the specific exercise and the individual athlete's muscular endurance. One athlete might need to hold a side plank for 90 seconds to reach an 8 or 9 out of 10 level of fatigue, while another might need just 30 seconds.

and purpose of the exercise and the strength of the individual athlete. In all cases, the aim is to 1) impose a load that fits the specific purpose of the exercise and 2) prescribe a number of repetitions or a duration that induces a high level of fatigue, but stops short of failure. The sidebar details basic load guidelines for each exercise type.

As for set numbers, research has shown that athletes get about 80 percent of the maximum possible benefit from any given strength exercise from just one set. This is good news for time-crunched athletes and for those who don't enjoy strength training. A second set will yield most of the remaining potential benefit of a given exercise, while a third set will finish the job. Elite endurance athletes seldom do more than three sets of any exercise in a single strength session.

Frequency, Timing, and Volume

Two sessions per week is the minimum requirement for gaining meaningful benefits from strength training. It is also close to the maximum frequency allowable before strength training begins to interfere with endurance training. Elite athletes in leg-dominant sports, such as cycling and running, typically limit themselves to two full-body strength workouts per week plus daily corrective exercise sessions. Elites in more strength-oriented endurance disciplines, including rowing, swimming, and cross-country skiing, often do three full-body strength sessions per week plus daily corrective exercise.

A typical duration for elite-style full-body strength workouts is one hour, while corrective exercise sessions generally last 20 to 30 minutes. This brings the total weekly time commitment to strength training to somewhere between 3 and 6 hours at the elite level. As mentioned previously, though, it is possible to gain significant benefits from a much smaller time investment. Athletes who have little time for, or interest in, strength training can save additional time either by folding their corrective exercises into their full-body strength workouts or by combining corrective exercises with mobility exercises, as indeed many elites do.

The best time to do full-body strength workouts is on the afternoon of a day that features a harder morning endurance workout. This minimizes the impact of fatigue produced by strength training on subsequent endurance training. Time-crunched recreational athletes should be encouraged to fit their strength workouts in whenever they can. After an initial adaptation period, most athletes find that they can make just about any schedule work as long as it is consistent. Following are examples of weekly strength training schedules that are appropriate for different categories of athletes, taking into account different sports and time commitments. If endurance training were superimposed on these schedules, key workouts would align with full-body strength sessions.

TABLE 8.1 **WEEKLY STRENGTH TRAINING FOR HIGHLY COMPETITIVE ENDURANCE ATHLETES***

MONDAY	TUESDAY	WEDNESDAY	THURSDAY	FRIDAY	SATURDAY	SUNDAY
CORRECTIVE EXERCISE 30:00	CORRECTIVE EXERCISE 30:00	CORRECTIVE EXERCISE 30:00	CORRECTIVE EXERCISE 30:00	CORRECTIVE EXERCISE 30:00	CORRECTIVE EXERCISE 30:00	CORRECTIVE EXERCISE 30:00
	FULL-BODY STRENGTH WORKOUT 30:00		FULL-BODY STRENGTH WORKOUT 30:00		FULL-BODY STRENGTH WORKOUT 30:00	

*Note: This group of athletes includes cross-country skiers, rowers, swimmers, cycling sprint specialists, and middle-distance runners.

TABLE 8.2 **WEEKLY STRENGTH TRAINING FOR HIGHLY COMPETITIVE CYCLISTS AND LONG-DISTANCE RUNNERS**

MONDAY	TUESDAY	WEDNESDAY	THURSDAY	FRIDAY	SATURDAY	SUNDAY
CORRECTIVE EXERCISE 30:00	CORRECTIVE EXERCISE 30:00	CORRECTIVE EXERCISE 30:00	CORRECTIVE EXERCISE 30:00	CORRECTIVE EXERCISE 30:00	CORRECTIVE EXERCISE 30:00	CORRECTIVE EXERCISE 30:00
	FULL-BODY STRENGTH WORKOUT 1:00:00			FULL-BODY STRENGTH WORKOUT 1:00:00		

TABLE 8.3 **WEEKLY STRENGTH TRAINING FOR BUSY ATHLETES***

MONDAY	TUESDAY	WEDNESDAY	THURSDAY	FRIDAY	SATURDAY	SUNDAY
CORRECTIVE + MOBILITY EXERCISE 20:00	FULL-BODY STRENGTH WORKOUT 45:00	CORRECTIVE + MOBILITY EXERCISE 20:00	CORRECTIVE + MOBILITY EXERCISE 20:00	FULL-BODY STRENGTH WORKOUT 45:00	CORRECTIVE + MOBILITY EXERCISE 20:00	CORRECTIVE + MOBILITY EXERCISE 20:00

*Note: This training schedule is also a good fit for athletes who don't enjoy strength training.

Progression, Periodization, and Variation

Keep in mind that strength training is not a primary but a secondary exercise modality for endurance athletes. As such, it is not an end in itself, but a means of supporting the athlete's endurance training (*principle of purpose*). For this reason, there is less emphasis placed on progression and periodization in the strength component of elite endurance training than there is in the endurance component. A build-and-maintain approach is more appropriate in strength training for endurance.

This is not to suggest that progression and periodization are completely lacking in the elite approach to strength training. They're just done in a relatively simple and straight-forward manner. Specifically, progression involves either increasing the load for a certain exercise that has become too easy for the athlete or replacing the exercise with a more challenging alternative. For example, if an athlete who starts off being able to complete 8 deadlifts at an effort level of 8 or 9 out of 10 with a load of 75 kilograms, then progresses to the point of being able to complete 10 repetitions at the same effort level, you might at this point add 10 kg to the load. Similarly, an athlete who starts off being able to complete 8 repetitions of the inverted row exercise at an effort level of 8 or 9 out of 10 and subsequently progresses to the point of being able to complete 15 repetitions at the same effort level might then advance to the more challenging pull-up exercise.

In most cases, it doesn't take very long for an athlete to make as much progress as they can with two to three gym sessions per week lasting 45 to 60 minutes each. At this point, the athlete's focus can shift to maintaining their gains and addressing specific weaknesses. To be clear, strength training should never become static, even after the athlete has reached a level where no further improvement is likely. Mixing up the exercise selection is one way to prevent stagnation. Strength adaptations are exercise-specific to some extent. An athlete who only does two-legged squats, for example, is likely to struggle with single-leg squats (*principle of specificity*). A well-designed strength program will feature a high degree of turnover in exercise selection and will routinely expose the athlete to new and unfamiliar exercises. Such variation is a subtle and underutilized way to make a strength program more challenging and effective over the long term. This method should not be taken to an extreme, however, as there is something to be said for featuring certain high-value exercises frequently in an individual athlete's strength program. This gives the athlete an opportunity to fully master these movements.

TABLE 8.4 **PERIODIZATION GUIDELINES FOR STRENGTH EXERCISES**

	OFF-SEASON	BASE PERIOD	PEAK PERIOD	TAPER PERIOD
Balance & Proprioceptive Exercises	Low	Moderate	Moderate	Low
Corrective Exercises	Moderate	Moderate	Moderate	Moderate
Explosive Movements	High	Moderate	High	Low
Functional Exercises	High	High	Moderate	Low
Heavy Lifts	High	High	Low	Low
Isometric Exercises	High	Moderate	Moderate	Low

○ LOW PRIORITY   ◐ MODERATE PRIORITY   ◐● HIGH PRIORITY

At the most general level, the strength component of an endurance athlete's training should be periodized in such a way that they do their most taxing strength workouts when their endurance training load is lightest and their least taxing strength workouts when their endurance training load is heaviest. In practical terms, this means strength training should be a higher priority during the off-season and base training periods than it is during the peak training and taper periods. These variations should not be drastic, however. As with progression, the *cyclicality principle* applies differently in these modalities than it does in endurance modalities. Unlike the endurance workouts you prescribe, strength workouts should remain fairly steady in frequency and duration throughout the year, except during brief post-season breaks. What variation there is in strength training emphasis should come mainly from manipulating the stress level of individual workouts. Table 8.4 offers basic periodization guidelines for the six types of strength exercises.

Sport Specificity

Cyclists should not strength train the same way as swimmers, who in turn should not strength train the same way as runners, and so forth. Although there are many exercises that are equally relevant and beneficial to athletes in all endurance disciplines, many others address the specific needs of athletes in just one or two sports. If you create strength programs for athletes in more than one endurance discipline, be sure to model the workouts on those that are done by elite athletes in the relevant sport (*principle of specificity*).

Individualization and Monitoring

Like endurance training, strength training must be prescribed in accordance with the *principle of individualization*. The main factors to consider when individualizing an athlete's strength program are (in addition to their sport) available equipment, recent and overall strength training experience, personal preferences, and weak areas.

Full gym access is always preferable in strength programming, as it allows the coach to select from the full panoply of relevant exercises. An effective program can be designed around inexpensive home equipment, however. In any case, you'll need to know what equipment the athlete has and doesn't have so you can plan accordingly.

Knowing the athlete's recent and overall strength training experience will help you meet the athlete where they are with the initial workouts you design for them. If the athlete has little or no strength training experience, it's best to start them off with workouts comprising a single set of a few simple exercises. "Simple" doesn't mean "easy." Strength workouts must be challenging to be beneficial, even for beginners. But a strength workout can be both hard and simple, and for athletes who are just starting out or starting over, the first phase of strength workouts should be made up of exercises that are easy to coordinate and execute with good form. An example is the **box squat**, a variation of the traditional squat that entails sitting down on a box positioned behind the athlete.

Age impacts strength training in a couple of different ways. Older athletes tend to be weaker than younger athletes and gain less strength in response to resistance exercise. Given these facts, you might think it's a good idea to prescribe higher volumes of strength training for older athletes than for younger athletes. But older athletes also take longer to recover from strength workouts, which are therefore more likely to interfere with endurance training in these athletes. So it's best to approach strength programming the same way for athletes of all ages.

Also consider athletes' preferences in planning their strength training. Athletes tend to be more invested in their training when they have a say in shaping it, and they also tend to enjoy it more. When athletes are invested in and enjoying their training, they get better results (*principle of enjoyment*). At the same time, you don't want to just hand the keys over to the athlete, as preferences aren't always consistent with best interests. In the gym, athletes often prefer exercises they're already good at or comfortable with, but they'll gain more from doing exercises they are less experienced and not comfortable with.

In addition to improving sport-specific strength, the strength training component of endurance training is meant to shore up individual weakness. Be aware of common weaknesses that are likely to be exposed in the course of executing a strength program:

- Relative lack of strength in particular muscles or movements compared to others (e.g., poor core strength)
- Lack of balance
- Lateral asymmetry (e.g., the right leg is stronger than the left)
- Poor neuromuscular coordination (evidenced by difficulty executing unfamiliar or complex movements)
- General non-responsiveness to strength training (the so-called hard gainer phenomenon)

Identifying such weaknesses requires active (and in most cases visual) monitoring of athletes while they work out. If you aren't able to watch your athletes in the gym, or if you lack the expertise to identify their individual weaknesses, you'll want to find a way to set them up with expert supervision, at least on a periodic basis.

Once identified, weaknesses can be addressed through heightened emphasis. For example, if you discover that an athlete's hip muscles are weaker on the left side than on the right, prescribe unilateral hip strengtheners, such as single-leg squats, and have the athlete do equal repetitions with equal loads on both sides, which initially will be much easier on the right leg. Other weaknesses can be addressed with a similar approach. An athlete who struggles with balance, to give another example, should be given more balance work than an athlete with exceptional balance.

Best Practices in Mobility Training for Endurance Sports

Mobility is important for endurance athletes because it enables them to perform athletic movements without restriction. Truth be told, there isn't a whole lot of science to support the purported benefits of mobility training, but scientific support isn't the only justification for adopting a method. The fact that mobility training is practiced almost universally by elite endurance athletes is justification enough. It's clearly not hurting athletes to work on mobility, and their own perception that mobility training enables them to move more freely during their endurance training is to be taken seriously. Any athlete who has gone from not doing mobility work to doing it regularly will tell you they feel better for it.

Most professional endurance athletes do mobility work at least once a day, often in combination with strength-based corrective exercises. These combined sessions are often done in the morning, as a way to "wake up" the body from overnight rest, but they are just as often done after endurance training. Some athletes like to do them in the evening as a way to wind down and work out the kinks after a hard day of training. There's really no bad time to do mobility work, though it is most effective after activity, when the body is primed for movement.

As mentioned, a typical elite-style mobility session takes 20 to 30 minutes to complete. As with strength training, any amount is better than none. When working with athletes who are reluctant to start a mobility training regimen, either because they feel they don't have the time or they aren't sold on the benefits, encourage them to do just enough to establish a habit, even if it's just one stretch a day. If you can get the athlete to take this first step, they are likely to discover that it feels good and volunteer to do more.

There are three basic types of exercise that improve mobility: static stretches, dynamic stretches, and myofascial release. **Static stretches** entail holding a muscle in a stretched position and are used to increase passive range of motion. **Dynamic stretches** entail moving a joint repeatedly through a full range of motion, which over time reduces internal resistance, allowing similar movements to be performed more comfortably and efficiently. **Myofascial release** is essentially self-massage using implements such as foam rollers, the purpose of which is to enhance muscle tissue pliability.

Mobility sessions may be either general or focused. A general routine is made up of six to ten exercises that cover the areas of the body that are most important for a particular sport. For example, a general mobility routine for swimmers will emphasize the shoulders, spine, and ankles, while a general mobility routine for runners will emphasize the hips, legs, and feet. Focused mobility sessions are typically shorter, comprising a handful of exercises targeting an individual athlete's specific limiters, the parts of the body that feel exceptionally tight or restricted, or that have been flagged by a physiotherapist as limiting.

The workout in the sidebar that follows is an example of a general mobility session for a triathlete that was pulled from one of the plans available at 8020endurance.com. Like the example of a full-body strength session offered earlier in this chapter (p. 124), it is intended for illustrative purposes only. Do not mistake it for a one-size-fits-all mobility routine appropriate for all athletes in all situations.

Each mobility exercise should be done in an amount that's sufficient to yield a palpable change in how that specific movement feels to the athlete. The minimum requirement for this effect is two sets lasting at least 20 seconds each, but many athletes will need to do more. Rest periods between sets should last just long enough for the athlete to feel the stretch clear itself from the affected muscles but no longer than half the duration of the preceding movement. For example, if the athlete is asked to hold a certain stretch for 18 seconds, the subsequent rest period should last up to 9 seconds. A well-paced mobility session has a nice flow to it but isn't hurried.

Each stretch included in a mobility session should be taken to the point of discomfort (POD), which is the first barrier of resistance the athlete feels as they settle into the stretch. Discomfort does not equal pain—*a stretch should never be painful*. The athlete should find that they are able to push back the POD in the later sets of a given stretch. It is common for athletes to develop a better feel for the right amount of stretch with experience.

Example of a General Mobility Session for a Triathlete

Links to video demonstrations of the individual exercises are available at 8020endurance.com.

EXERCISE	SETS / REPS
Hamstring Hurdler	2 sets of 30 seconds per side
Frog Stretch	2 sets of 8 reps (back and forth)
Anterior Hip Stretch with Band	2 sets of 30 seconds per side
Quad Wall Stretch	2 sets of 30 seconds per side
Talus Mobilization	2 sets of 12 reps
Big Toe Elevated Calf Stretch	2 sets of 8 reps (in and out)
Runner's Lunge	2 sets of 30 seconds per side
T4 Rotation	2 sets of 6 reps per side
Praying Squat	2 sets of 20 seconds

Progression is a natural outcome of the process. The same basic routine, repeated over and over, will result in mobility gains that the athlete can then reinvest in the process by moving deeper into the various stretches that make up the routine. Additional progress can be stimulated by lengthening stretches, adding sets and reps, and adding movements.

DON'T REINVENT THE WHEEL

We close this chapter with a reminder that you don't have to become a full-blown expert on strength and mobility training to meet the ancillary training needs of the athletes you coach. There are lots of good resources you can lean on to make up for what you lack. Among these are the ready-made strength and mobility programs that are available for use by all 80/20 Endurance–certified coaches and accessible to all athletes. Even the greatest coaches incorporate smart strategies and sessions from other coaches. Don't be shy about doing the same, while being attentive to how individual athletes respond.

Coaching for Race-Day Success

⟋ Coaches can set athletes up for successful racing by assisting them in race selection, goal setting, course-specific preparation, pacing, race nutrition, and mindset.

⟋ Race goals should be finalized within the final two weeks before competition so that they can be based on the most current data. Once they have been set, such goals should be pushed out of mind and the focus should turn to execution.

⟋ The most important element of race execution is pacing. Athletes should have a sensible and specific pacing plan for every race and should practice pacing in training.

⟋ Every race, good or bad, is a learning experience. Take time after each race to thoroughly analyze the athlete's performance with them, teasing out lessons that can be applied in the next race.

The global pandemic of 2020 reminded endurance athletes all over the world of something that many had previously taken for granted, which is that they train for the sake of competing. Make no mistake—the training process offers a number of intrinsic rewards. However, when all of the races suddenly went away most athletes languished to some degree, no longer seeing much point in working out. Racing is always hard, often nerve-wracking, and sometimes disappointing, yet it is also what gives the athletic journey meaning (*principle of purpose*).

As you know, the job of an endurance coach is to help athletes achieve their goals, and the goals that athletes pursue are almost always race-related. Planning, monitoring, and adjusting training accounts for the bulk of the work a coach does to prepare their athletes for race-day success, but not the entirety of it. A different set of coaching responsibilities comes to the fore in the final days and hours before competition. In this chapter, we will offer guidance concerning a number of these responsibilities, including race selection, goal setting, course-specific preparation, pacing, race nutrition, and mindset.

One thing that is important to keep in mind as you prepare your athletes to compete is that you cannot race *for* them, nor should you want to. There comes a time in every coach-athlete partnership when the athlete is on their own, and it's up to them to do what it takes to succeed. Few experiences in the life of a coach are more gratifying than that of seeing an athlete succeed on their own, without outside help. The best coaches develop athletes who don't need their coach when the starting horn sounds. This chapter will equip you with some of the tools to develop such athletes.

Race Selection

It has been said that racing is the enemy of training. What is meant by this statement is that racing is highly disruptive to the training process, requiring significant reductions in load both before and after each event. It is therefore impossible to race often and train consistently, and it is equally impossible to train inconsistently and race well. Any endurance athlete who wants to perform well when they race should race sparingly, if possible.

We say "if possible" because not all athletes have the option to race sparingly. Those who compete for teams or clubs with fixed schedules might find themselves racing as often as once a week during the competitive season. The best way to manage this type of schedule as a coach is to treat races as workouts (i.e., as time spent at moderate/high intensity) for planning purposes. Think of them as a series of hard training sessions that you need to incorporate into a program that enables your athletes to perform at their highest level in the most important events later in the season. To maximize your chances of succeeding in this effort, use the pre-season period to develop a high level of general fitness in your athletes. Your aim here is to get them fit enough to handle the frequent racing to come, but not so fit that the races themselves won't make them even fitter. During the season, create balance around races by planning key workouts that target intensities both higher and lower than race intensity and also by including enough rest and recovery to prevent overreaching (*principle of balance*).

Athletes who get to choose their own races enjoy greater freedom to compete at opportune moments. The most opportune moment is the end of a macrocycle, when the athlete is in a state of high fitness and low fatigue resulting from having gradually built their training load to their personal sweet spot and then tapered. The least opportune period for racing is the early part of the macrocycle, when the athlete has not yet reached a level of fitness that enables them to meet or exceed their performance standards. Between these two points—the point when the athlete is fit enough to race successfully and the end of the training cycle, when they are ready to perform at peak level in their "A" race—is a good time for one or more "B" races. Athletes specializing in shorter events, which require less recovery time, are generally able to complete several races of secondary importance within this window without disrupting their training excessively. Athletes specializing in the longer events might only be able to do one "B" race ahead of their "A" race. This is all the more true for runners, who typically need more time to recover from races.

For the most part, coaches should allow, and even encourage, athletes to take the lead in selecting races. It's their sport, after all, and they have the right to choose the goals that get them most excited. They also tend to work harder and improve more when allowed to choose their own races (*principle of enjoyment*). Just be ready to step in when an athlete's preferences don't serve their best interests. Left to their own devices, many recreational endurance athletes race at inopportune times or simply too often. If you see an athlete heading down this path, explain why it's not a good idea and steer them toward better choices.

Athletes who like to race often are good candidates for adopting the acyclic method of periodization described in Chapter 5. This "always ready" approach to training gives athletes the flexibility to compete relatively frequently for a period of time without undue risk of nonfunctional overreaching. Even with this approach, however, an athlete cannot just keep going and going. At least once every six months there should be a short reset where the athlete returns to base training, and at least once a year the athlete should take a full break from training (*principle of cyclicality*).

Elite athletes are financially incentivized to race often but never poorly. This is a good example to follow. By studying the race schedules of the most successful pros you will get an idea of how to strike the same balance with your athletes. Following are two examples of sensible race schedules for athletes who, like the professionals, wish to race as often as they are able to perform at their best. Table 9.1 is for a runner aiming at a marathon "A" race, while Table 9.2 is for a triathlete who takes an acyclic approach to training for Olympic-distance events.

TABLE 9.1 **RACE SCHEDULE FOR A RUNNER**

WEEK 1	2	3	4	5	6	7	8	9	10	11	12	13	14	15	16	17	18
								5K			10K			Half-Marathon			Marathon

- The runner's schedule assumes a traditional approach to periodization, where the macrocycle begins after an off-season break and builds to a single peak. The first eight weeks, therefore, are devoted to base training, or building the athlete's fitness from a relatively low level to the threshold of race-readiness.
- The specific order of the runner's four races is sensible. It doesn't take as long to get fit for shorter races as it does to get fit for longer races, so whenever an athlete's "A" race is on the longer side, it's a good idea to arrange the preceding events in order of increasing distance.
- The runner's races have been scheduled for times when the runner would likely be due for a recovery week. This minimizes the races' disruptiveness to the flow of training. We can assume that each race is both preceded and followed by a few days of lighter training.

TABLE 9.2 **RACE SCHEDULE FOR A SHORT-COURSE TRIATHLETE**

WEEK 1	2	3	4	5	6	7	8	9	10	11	12	13	14	15	16	17	18
Race			Race		Race						Race			Race			Race

- The triathlete's schedule assumes an acyclic approach to periodization. This athlete's base-building period will have preceded the 18-week racing phase shown in the table.
- It's not easy to perform at a peak level in six Olympic-distance triathlons in a span of 18 weeks. To succeed in this ambition, the triathlete will need to do a reset in Weeks 7–8, during which they return to easy base training. Done correctly, this short breather will rejuvenate the athlete enough to perform at or near a peak level in the remaining three races of the season.

These are just two examples selected from an infinite number we might have put forward. Planning race schedules for athletes is not a matter of choosing from a handful of acceptable templates but of creating something original for each situation. The possibilities are limitless, but at the same time they are constrained by basic principles and proven practices that, if heeded, will enable you to avoid mistakes in race planning.

Finalizing Race Goals

The topic of goal setting was covered in Chapter 6, but we'd like to return to it here to underscore a couple of important points and offer additional guidance. The key thing to remember about race outcome goals is that their main purpose is to stretch the athlete to their highest level of performance. This requires that the goals be just barely achievable, which in turn requires that goals must be based on an accurate estimate of the athlete's performance potential. It's advisable, therefore, to wait until a week or two before race day to finalize outcome goals. Training data from key workouts performed in the last and hardest weeks of training are more reliable as predictors of race performance than training data from workouts done earlier in the macrocycle. It's okay, and often useful, to set provisional goals at or near the beginning of the cycle. Doing so can motivate an athlete to make maximum progress throughout the training process, but it's important that neither the athlete nor the coach set their heart on these goals, which are likely to require revision when the process is near completion.

With goal setting comes pressure. Pressure is a doubled-edged sword that, in the right circumstances, aids performance. In the wrong circumstances it may do the opposite, causing an athlete to choke. A sure way to keep pressure from harming an athlete's performance is to set low expectations, but it's much better to set high expectations. Encourage athletes to welcome the pressure that comes with high expectations, as well as the opportunity to excel that comes with pressure—as the saying goes, "Pressure is a privilege." As a coach, you can further reduce the risk of your athletes choking in an event by fostering a healthy perspective on their goals.

Remind your athletes, as often as necessary, that it truly does not matter whether they achieve the time they want or finish in the position they want. What does matter is how well they control the things that are within their control, of which there are three: effort, attitude, and decisions. An athlete who finishes a race knowing they gave their best effort, kept a positive attitude, and made smart decisions has every reason to be satisfied with their performance, regardless of whether their primary outcome goal was achieved. True success, in other words, is a race well-executed, and execution is entirely within the athlete's control, hence no cause for worry. Keeping athletes focused on what they do during the race, rather than on where they rank at the end of the race, has a potent calming effect on athletes who are prone to pre-race performance anxiety.

Research has found that athletes tend to achieve better outcomes when they focus on execution. That's one more reason to encourage the athletes you coach to do so. "Run the mile you're in," is another useful sports adage. An athlete should not think about the finish line until they cross it, as looking ahead distracts the athlete from the task at hand, and it is by concentrating on the task at hand that they get to the finish line most quickly.

The most effective way to keep athletes focused on execution both before and during races is to equip them with a concrete race plan made up of specific, relevant process goals. Keep in mind that a race plan is not a race script. To perform optimally in races, athletes must be clear-minded, flexible, and responsive. An excessively detailed or rigid plan will deprive the athlete of the autonomy they need to handle the surprises that every race presents. Here's an example of a sensible set of process goals for a triathlete hoping to podium in their age group:

SWIM: Get out fast and try to draft off a strong swimmer with good sighting skills.

First transition: Tune out the clock and the other competitors and focus on the steps you rehearsed in training.

BIKE: Stay at or below 275 watts for the first 20 minutes, then assess how you feel and push a little harder if you've got good legs. Drink every 10 minutes.

Second transition: Increase your cadence and stand out of the saddle to stretch your legs and back as you approach the transition area entrance. Don't panic if something goes wrong. Swallow a gel packet as you exit.

RUN: Ignore your watch for the first minute as you find your running legs, then settle into your target pace of 4:20/km. Pretend every athlete in front of you is a competitor in your age group, whether they are or aren't. Make a game of counting how many you pass.

RACE PLAN TEMPLATE

PERFORMANCE GOAL(S)
Finish time/place, segment times. Consider setting secondary and tertiary goals the athlete can fall back on if things don't go their way.

PACING PLAN
This can include an overall pacing plan for the race and segmental plans for different parts of the race. See the section on pacing for further guidance.

NUTRITION PLAN
Execute the science-based fueling strategy practiced in training. See the section on nutrition for further guidance.

MENTAL CUES
These can include anything from mantras ("Stay relaxed") to cues for attentional focus ("Sight every 6 strokes during the swim")—anything the athlete can do with their thoughts and feelings to enhance their performance and race experience.

TACTICAL PLAN
Plans for using the course and other racers to one's own advantage. See the section on pacing for further guidance.

There is no single set of execution goals that applies to every athlete and every event. Each race plan you create should be unique, tailored to the individual athlete and a specific race. Think pragmatically, aiming to devise the most concise set of instructions sufficient to position the athlete for success. The Race Plan Template (p. 141) serves as a framework for creating individualized race plans for athletes.

To recap, here's our recommended approach to setting race goals with athletes:

1. Set firm performance goals when the race is close enough that all relevant information concerning the athlete's fitness and race conditions is available.
2. Set outcome goals that both you and the athlete believe will be difficult, but not impossible, to achieve.
3. Once these goals are set, encourage the athlete to put them out of mind and focus entirely on race execution.

Race-Specific Preparation

An important part of preparing athletes for competitive success is getting them ready for the specific course and conditions they will encounter on race day (*principle of specificity*). A 10K running race that takes place on a track at sea level on a cool evening, for example, is very different from a 10K running race that goes from the bottom to the top of a technical trail at high elevation in summer heat. An athlete who prepares simply to run a fast 10K and enters the latter event is likely to perform poorly due to lack of specific preparation for the course and conditions.

Topography and Terrain

To avoid leaving athletes feeling underprepared on race day, ensure that a portion of their training is specific to the course of their next important event. If the course is hilly, the athlete should perform some workouts on hilly routes. If the course involves an ocean swim, the athlete should do some ocean swims in training. Granted, this is sometimes easier said than done. An athlete who lives in central Florida won't have an easy time finding hills to train on, and an athlete living in southern Germany will have a difficult time finding an ocean to swim in. In cases like these, plan one or two special excursions to areas that have race-specific geography to build the athlete's confidence.

If the athlete has the ability to train on the actual race course, so much the better. Such familiarization is valuable for a number of reasons. First, it helps set appropriate expectations, as more often than not, the course is tougher than expected. It also forestalls unpleasant surprises, provides information for race strategy, reduces pre-race anxiety, and lowers the cognitive strain of racing in unfamiliar territory. If training on the race course is not feasible, look at alternatives such as touring the course by car, watching a video course tour, or studying route maps.

Climate and Weather

The same principles that govern preparation for individual race courses apply to preparing for specific conditions. An athlete preparing for a triathlon that will feature a swim in very cold water should practice swimming in very cold water at least a couple of times before the event. The most challenging special conditions that athletes commonly encounter in races are heat and altitude. Training in hot environments stimulates physiological adaptations that enhance performance, not only in similar environments but in all conditions, meaning every athlete would benefit from including it in their training.

It takes approximately ten days to get the full benefit of heat training, and the adaptations recede quickly after exposure. The most straightforward way to carry the benefits of heat training into competition is to combine it with a ten-day pre-race taper. This ensures the desired adaptations are fresh, and because the training load is reduced during the taper period, the physiological strain of heat training is lower than it would be during periods of heavier training. Another option is to have the athlete perform two or three heat training sessions per week over a period of several weeks. These sessions may take any form. Easy workouts will suffice if the cumulative exposure is adequate. There is an additional psychological benefit to be gained by doing one or two race-specific workouts in the heat if you believe your athletes are ready for the challenge (i.e., if the athlete has previously shown strong tolerance for easy workouts in the heat).

High Elevation

The best way to prepare for a race at high elevation is to spend at least two weeks living and training at high elevation prior to competing. However, this is often impractical for athletes living at lower elevations. The next best thing is arriving at the race site a couple of days early. Meaningful physiological adaptations to oxygen-poor air occur within 72 hours. Athletes should have their blood ferritin level checked before traveling to high elevations and consider taking supplemental iron to prepare the body for the drain on iron stores that comes with visiting the mountains.

Don't Overdo It

In helping athletes prepare for specific race courses and conditions, be careful to avoid trying to control everything. Efforts to do so are not only doomed to fail but are likely to create unnecessary anxiety in the athlete. It's better to be 91 percent prepared and calm than 97 percent prepared and freaking out about the uncontrollable 3 percent. Athletes pick up emotional cues from coaches the way pets do from their human guardians. By all means, be detail-oriented in preparing athletes for competition, but maintain a healthy perspective. If you seem anxious, your athletes will notice and become anxious too.

Race Pacing

Pacing is arguably the most important component of race execution. In each and every race, a certain fraction of an athlete's performance potential is wasted due to imperfect pacing. The average runner, for example, loses more than four minutes over the course of completing a marathon as a result of pacing errors. The more skillfully an athlete paces a given race, the closer they get to realizing 100 percent of their performance potential on that day.

Despite the critical importance of pacing to overall race execution, most endurance athletes put little thought into their pacing strategy for individual events. One of the most important responsibilities of a coach in the final days before a race is helping the athlete formulate a pacing plan. Long before that point, ensure the athlete understands what constitutes good pacing so they can practice it in training. The defining characteristic of a well-paced race is consistency. Large variations in output hasten fatigue. Highly skilled pacers quickly find the highest output they can sustain over the full distance and maintain it the entire way.

Here's the fine print: Slightly different pacing patterns appear to be optimal in different events. In middle-distance running events the best performances are associated with a U-shaped pacing pattern, where the first and last parts of the race are a bit faster than the middle part. In ultramarathons there is a gradual slowing pattern over the latter part of the race, even among the highest performers. It must be emphasized, however, that these are modest departures from consistency. The main difference between the pacing of high performers and everyone else is that the high performers are more consistent.

Because good pacing is all about consistency, it's important that athletes start each race knowing their highest sustainable output for the distance or duration of the event. Note that output and pace are not the same thing. It is actually a steady output, or rate of energy expenditure, not a steady pace, or speed, that leads to perfect pacing. In a race with variable terrain or conditions, a steady output will not yield a steady pace but it will yield the fastest possible finish for the athlete.

Power is the purest measure of output. Cyclists who race on bikes equipped with a power meter are able to go into their races with a target wattage that represents their estimated highest sustainable output. They can then monitor their power throughout the race to ensure consistency. But in other types of events, such as skimo races, output monitoring is impossible and athletes must find their highest sustainable output by feel.

No problem. Even when direct or indirect output monitoring is possible, skillful pacing is ultimately done by feel. That's because endurance performance is limited by perception of effort, not by physiology. When an athlete reaches a point where they *feel* they cannot continue at their present level of output, they're right regardless of what's going on inside them physiologically. The true goal of pacing, then, is to produce a gradually increasing level of perceived effort that peaks when the athlete is approaching the finish line. Output monitoring can aid this process, but studies have demonstrated that experienced athletes pace just as well without it. Overreliance on data can artificially limit performance by deflecting attention from the perceptions that ultimately determine an athlete's true limit.

The most skilled pacers ask themselves continuously throughout each race, "Is this effort sustainable?" Three factors help them answer this question accurately. The first is a deeply ingrained habit of asking this very question, which over time gives athletes the ability to read their perceptions with remarkable nuance. The second factor, which is related to the first, is experience. The more races an athlete has completed, the better they know how they should feel at various points in any given race. The third factor is explicit knowledge of what lies ahead in the race currently being undertaken. The more the athlete knows about the race course and conditions, the more informed their sustainability estimates will be. As a coach, you can help your athletes feel their way to optimal pacing in races by getting them in the habit of asking themselves, "Is this effort sustainable?" in both workouts and races and by making sure they have a thorough knowledge of the course and conditions of each race.

The race pacing guidelines we've offered up to this point assume that the athlete is racing for time rather than for position. While the two objectives are not mutually exclusive, they demand different strategical approaches. The keys to racing successfully for position are 1) playing to one's strengths, 2) using other athletes to one's own advantage, and 3) not allowing oneself to be used to other athletes' advantage. When you're coaching an athlete who will be competing for position rather than for time in an upcoming race, you'll want to work with them to develop a strategy that considers these three elements.

Race Nutrition

Nutrition plays a significant role in longer events. Fueling is unnecessary and potentially counterproductive in races lasting less than one hour. For events that exceed this threshold, it is imperative that your athletes have a specific and well-rehearsed fueling plan. Some coaches like to farm out this type of guidance to an experienced sports nutrition professional, but every endurance coach should at least understand the basics of race fueling. The sidebar on page 147 details the most important guidelines for nutrition intake during endurance competition.

It is vitally important that athletes practice their race fueling in training. Informal practice is achieved through everyday workout fueling, but prior to each race athletes should perform a couple of highly race-specific workouts before and during which they fuel exactly as they intend to do on race day. Additionally, athletes preparing for multi-hour events will benefit from working to increase their tolerance for nutrition intake during exercise. This practice of gut training entails consuming incrementally increasing amounts of fluids and carbohydrates in a series of longer workouts.

Handling Logistics

Logistics aren't the most glamorous part of race preparation, but they are another important part. Many an athlete has allowed a race to be ruined by failure to set an alarm, transportation and parking snafus, forgotten equipment, accidental rule violations, etc. Depending on the type of coaching you do, helping your athletes with pre-race logistics might or might

GUIDELINES FOR RACE-DAY NUTRITION

Athletes should **DRINK** ad libitum (i.e., as desired) at intervals of 10 to 20 minutes throughout races lasting longer than 60 to 70 minutes. The exact amount should depend on thirst and gastrointestinal comfort.

Athletes who tend not to be mindful of their thirst should get in the habit of drinking on a regular schedule (again, every 10 to 20 minutes) in key workouts and races.

Athletes should consume **CARBO-HYDRATES** at a rate of 60 to 90 grams per hour in races lasting between 1 and 2.5 hours and at a rate of 90 to 120 grams per hour during races lasting longer than 2.5 hours.

The best sources of carbohydrate are sports drinks, carbohydrate gels and chews, and other products containing a combination of multiple carbohydrate types. Whole foods are less effective but are better tolerated by some athletes.

FAT should not be consumed in competition except by those athletes who seem to tolerate their overall nutrition intake better with the inclusion of some fat during races. Small amounts of protein or amino acids may be helpful in reducing muscle damage and its performance impact during multi-hour races.

Athletes should try to meet their total race fueling needs with as few sources as possible. In other words, fueling plans should be as simple as possible.

Solid foods are best avoided, except in extremely long events in which hunger is likely to become a distraction.

CAFFEINE consumed one hour before race time, in the amount of 3 to 6 milligrams per kilogram of bodyweight, will enhance performance in most athletes. Consuming caffeine in smaller amounts during races may further enhance performance.

Athletes prone to **GI DISTRESS** during races often need to experiment with different carbohydrate sources to find the one(s) they tolerate best. Discourage athletes from concluding prematurely that recommended levels of carbohydrate intake are unattainable for them just because they've had a bad reaction to a single product.

not fall within the scope of your responsibilities. Either way, your responsibilities, and the limits thereof, should be clearly understood on both sides. To the extent that you accept responsibility for assisting with pre-race logistics, carry out your duties with diligence.

Specific tasks you may choose to handle or assist the athlete with include creating a race gear checklist, bike shipping and setup, creating a race-morning itinerary, planning race-day transit and parking, race packet pickup, gear and/or nutrition drop-off, transition walkthrough, and support crew service. Your overall approach to pre-race logistics should strike a careful balance between thoroughness and calmness. If you're not thorough enough, lapses are likely. On the other hand, if you fuss excessively over every little detail, you risk conveying an implicit message that absolute control is necessary for success. This could cause the athlete to panic the moment they realize they can't control everything.

Competitive Mindset

Athletes must be ready to race not only physically and logistically, but also mentally. Pre-competition mental states have been extensively studied. Researchers consistently find that certain states (stress, apathy) harm performance while others (confidence, eagerness) enhance it. As a coach, you are not responsible for getting your athletes into the right mindset for optimal performance before races. Athletes need to be able to do this for themselves, and all the more so because the optimal mindset varies between individuals. For example, some athletes like to race angry, while others prefer a grateful mindset. What you can do is assist with an athlete's own efforts to adopt the right mindset before races. The three most effective ways to nurture this mindset are to 1) ensure the athlete has a clear path to success, 2) remind the athlete that they *want* to race, and 3) help the athlete maintain a process focus.

Ensure the athlete has a clear path to success.

It is essential that your athletes have a clear definition of success when looking ahead to a race, and that they believe success is likely. They must also have a plan that empowers them to achieve success by their own efforts. When these conditions are in place, athletes approach the race with a feeling of eager anticipation that is conducive to performance. When one or more of these conditions are absent, athletes tend to feel stressed out about or unmotivated for competition.

An athlete doesn't have to be in the best shape of their life to have a successful race. The most common mistake athletes make when entering a race with less-than-perfect form is failing to define success in a way that's realistic. All too often, they refuse to adjust their expectations to account for a setback or some other factor that places their original goal out of reach. Athletes prone to black-and-white thinking around success need to be coaxed to accept shades of gray. A sure sign of a mature athlete is the ability to look back on a race and say, "That was pretty good, *all things considered*." Your task is to help athletes consider all things relevant to defining success for a given race.

Remind the athlete that they want to race.

At the beginning of this chapter, we mentioned how the global pandemic of 2020 reminded many athletes that they genuinely want to race. When a race is imminent, however, athletes often behave as if they *don't* want to race, as fears of discomfort and failure kick in. These fears don't actually erase the desire to compete but merely mask it. In communicating with nervous athletes in the days before a race, find gentle ways to remind them that they really do want to compete, to experience the discomfort of racing, and to risk failure, all of which is true. Racing is a free choice the athlete has made because they love their sport and because they feel good about themselves when they face discomfort and the possibility of failure by giving their best effort.

To be clear, you're not trying to convince the nervous athlete to accept *your* beliefs about racing. You're merely putting them back in touch with their own beliefs. The goal is not to cancel their fears, but to allow these fears to coexist with their genuine desire to race.

Help the athlete maintain a process focus.

Coaches should waste very little time and energy in discussing goals with athletes in the days before a race. What good does it do? Once an appropriate goal has been set, there's nothing more to say about it. Thinking and talking about goals after they've been set serves no purpose except to generate anxiety and distract the athlete from the race experience. Coaches should make a point of keeping their pre-race communications with athletes focused on the process that will lead to a successful outcome rather than on the outcome itself. Doing so not only helps keep the athlete's focus where it should be, but it also has a calming effect. "Coach doesn't seem worried, so why should I worry?"

Post-Race Analysis

Every endurance athlete has good races and bad races. A certain amount of risk is inherent in the effort to perform at the absolute limit of one's ability, and that is as it should be. People don't become endurance athletes because they want a guarantee; they become endurance athletes because they want a challenge, and no endeavor that is truly challenging comes with a 100-percent success rate.

All races, good and bad, present equal opportunity for learning. Athletes should not merely celebrate successful races and regret unsuccessful outings. Win or lose, they should also reflect on their performance, identifying the things they did well and the things they did poorly, with a view toward applying the lessons of this particular race to the next one. As a coach, you are in an excellent position to help athletes in this process.

The most straightforward approach to post-race analysis is the chronological narrative. The athlete walks their coach through the race from beginning to end and the coach chimes in with questions and comments intended to highlight good decisions that should be replicated in future races and bad decisions that should be corrected. There's always emotion involved when an athlete is reviewing a recent race. It's best to be as objective and dispassionate as possible when conducting this exercise, almost as if you and the athlete are reviewing someone else's performance. It's too late to change the outcome of the race, but it's not too late to maximize the race's utility, which requires clear-eyed, honest dissection.

The benefits of post-race analysis are threefold. First, it gives athletes an opportunity to process the experience emotionally. Racing is intense, and athletes need to talk about what they went through to gain closure before they are ready to move on. Second, as mentioned previously, a post-race analysis also transforms the experience into learning. Athletes do not automatically execute their next race more skillfully just because they've added one more competitive outing to their trove of experience. Unless a race is studied and evaluated after completion, some of its potential teachings go unlearned. And third, conducting a formal analysis with your athletes makes racing less risky, in a sense, by ensuring that it contributes to their betterment, regardless of the outcome. When athletes regard each race not as a final chance to do their best, but as a stepping-stone toward better racing in the future, they're more relaxed and less likely to choke under pressure.

Coaching
the Mind

⊿ There is a psychological dimension to coaching endurance athletes that cannot be overlooked. The most practical way for coaches to handle this part of the job is to use the normal process of solving training-related problems to help athletes develop mental fitness, which we define as the ability to make the best of a bad situation.

⊿ The most mentally fit athletes make the best of bad situations through a three-step process of accepting, embracing, and addressing reality. The coach's role in training the mind is to guide athletes through this process when problems arise.

⊿ The widely used counseling practice of motivational interviewing provides a framework that coaches can use to help athletes fully face reality and develop mental fitness in the course of solving problems that arise in training and competition.

ndurance racing is famously challenging, not just physically but also mentally. All sports are mentally challenging to some degree, but only in endurance racing is performance directly limited by psychology. Remember, an endurance race is, by definition, a paced event where athletes deliberately maintain a submaximal output to avoid hitting their physical limit prematurely. In a well-paced race, the athlete does not encounter any kind of physical limit until they are within sight of the finish line. Prior to that point, they are *feeling* their way toward their limit using perceived effort, a purely psychological phenomenon that rises to painfully intense levels in the latter part of a properly executed race.

Managing perceived effort is but one aspect of the psychological dimension of the endurance sports experience. Various mental challenges confront athletes almost daily in the course of training. These range from dips in motivation to concerns about fitness to disappointment over bad workouts. Some athletes manage the mental challenges they face in training and competition more effectively than others do, but very few consistently manage these challenges as well as they possibly could. Put another way, at any given time, most endurance athletes are holding themselves back mentally in one way or another.

Helping athletes to manage these common challenges more effectively is an important responsibility for coaches. It's okay—more than okay—to encourage athletes to work with a sports psychologist or a mental performance coach to improve their mental game. Unlike nutrition and strength training, however, a coach cannot realistically delegate all responsibility for handling the psychological dimension of the sport. There is a psychological aspect to everything an athlete does and to every interaction you have with each athlete. It is imperative, therefore, that you handle this part of your coaching role strategically and intentionally. This does not mean you have to actually become a sports psychologist yourself. It just means you need to know how to coach the mind.

As we saw in Chapter 6, helping athletes address sport-related problems is a primary responsibility of the coach. The interactions that occur around problem solving are natural opportunities for coaches to cultivate mental fitness in athletes. This is done by guiding the athlete through the process that the most mentally fit athletes use to overcome problems of all kinds. With this approach, coaches are able to contribute to their athletes' mental fitness development without stepping outside the normal coaching role, hence outside their area of competence.

The goal of this chapter is to describe a concrete process that endurance coaches can use to develop mental fitness through practical problem solving. Our first step will be to define mental fitness in a manner that provides a clear understanding of what you are trying to achieve in coaching the mind. We will then describe and illustrate a particular approach to practical problem solving and mental fitness development that is based on a form of cognitive-behavioral therapy called reality therapy, which is the approach we recommend for 80/20 Endurance coaches. Ultimately, mastery is the goal behind all goals in endurance sport participation and of the coach, who acts as a facilitator of the pursuit of mastery, particularly as this relates to mental fitness development.

Training Mental Fitness

We define mental fitness as the ability to make the best of a bad situation. A bad situation, in turn, can be defined as any situation in which goal attainment has become more difficult than expected or hoped. What distinguishes this definition of mental fitness from most others is that it is operational, meaning it describes mental fitness in terms of what it *does* rather than in terms of the qualities that comprise it (e.g., resilience). An athlete who consistently makes the best of the bad situations they encounter has a high level of mental fitness by our definition, whereas an athlete who consistently fails to make the best of the bad situations they encounter has a low level of mental fitness. This point of distinction is important because it affects how mental fitness is developed. When mental fitness is defined in terms of its constituent qualities, it is developed through the cultivation of these qualities. But when it is defined in terms of how it functions, mental fitness is developed by emulating what athletes with high levels of mental fitness do.

The next question is this: *How do athletes make the best of bad situations?* The answer is simple: by fully facing the reality of these situations. There are three steps involved in the process of fully facing the reality of a bad situation: accepting, embracing, and addressing.

Step 1: Accept reality. To accept the reality of a bad situation is to perceive it in a way that preserves one's ability to make choices. In other words, acceptance means recognizing that the situation is unlikely to change for the better unless the athlete changes it for themself. Failure to accept the reality of a bad situation occurs when an athlete keeps wishing it hadn't occurred, denies it has occurred, or hopes it changes on its own.

Step 2: Embrace reality. To embrace the reality of a bad situation is to commit to making the best of it, even if the best that can be realistically made of it isn't all that much better than the present reality. Moving from acceptance to embracing means pivoting from acknowledging the problem to seeking a solution. Failure to embrace the reality of a bad situation occurs when an athlete becomes demoralized or apathetic in the face of it.

Step 3: Address the problem. To address a bad situation is to do the actual work required to make the best of it. In the language of a familiar expression, addressing a bad situation means doing everything in one's power to turn lemons into lemonade. Failure to address a bad situation occurs when an athlete either doesn't try as hard as they could or doesn't exercise their best judgment in pursuit of the best possible outcome.

Reality Therapy

Bad situations come in almost infinite varieties. An athlete succeeds in making the best of such a situation by first accepting their present reality, then embracing it, and lastly addressing it. The coach's role in these situations is to guide athletes through these three steps. As mentioned above, this approach is rooted in *reality therapy*, a psychotherapeutic method developed by psychiatrist William Glasser in the 1960s as a way to help people make responsible decisions that are consistent with their values and grounded in a clear understanding of reality.

You don't have to be a licensed therapist to practice this technique effectively. In essence, it's nothing more than a formalized method of doing what good coaches do intuitively in the normal course of interacting with athletes. But that doesn't mean it's easy. To the contrary, practicing reality therapy is quite challenging, as a number of powerful instincts tend to block our ability to fully face reality, especially in difficult situations. As the psychiatrist Robert Trivers wrote, "The human capacity for self-deception knows no bounds." Getting your athletes to the point where fully facing reality in bad situations comes naturally is likely to require patient and persistent nudging on your part over a long period of time. And that's okay. After all, maximizing physical fitness is a slow process that takes a while to complete. Why would we expect it to be any different with mental fitness?

Motivational Interviewing

Don't be intimidated by the word "therapy." All you're really doing in helping athletes accept, embrace, and address reality is communicating with them. Specifically, you're having structured, purposeful conversations in which you assume a steering role. The widely used, evidence-based method of motivational interviewing offers coaches a simple playbook to draw from in these conversations. Originally used to treat alcohol addiction, motivational interviewing differs from some other counseling methods in that it is more collaborative and client-centered. As such, it's a great way to practice reality therapy, which shares the same insistence on treating clients as autonomous adults who are fully capable of taking responsibility for their own behavior.

In the coaching context, *motivational interviewing* employs nine techniques that coaches can use to steer their conversations with athletes in the right direction. Together, they represent a complete toolkit that is applicable to the problems athletes normally encounter in training and racing. We will describe these techniques and share examples of how to apply them to common mental obstacles faced by endurance athletes, including loss of motivation, performance anxiety, and self-doubt.

Explain your approach to problem solving and mental fitness development.

Treating athletes as autonomous, responsible adults during the process of helping them accept, embrace, and address the reality of a bad situation begins with letting them know exactly what you're doing. There is no reason to hide the therapeutic concepts you're applying with them; in fact, you have every reason to share them explicitly. Explain what mental fitness is, the goal of reality therapy, and how motivational interviewing works. (While you're at it, encourage the athlete to read *The Comeback Quotient*.) The last thing you want your athletes to experience in your problem-solving conversations with them is a sense of being manipulated in the service of some unspoken agenda. The process will be far more efficient if athletes understand and buy into the conceptual framework you're using.

Ask your athlete to define the problem they're experiencing.

Athletes often misidentify the problems they face. In other words, what they think is the problem is very often not the actual problem. Consider the example of loss of motivation for an event goal. When this happens, athletes tend to assume that the problem is lack of motivation itself. You hear them say things like, "I don't know what's wrong with me! I need to get my motivation back!" But in many cases the real problem is that the athlete feels obligated to want something they no longer want. And when this is the case, the solution lies not in restoring motivation but in accepting that the goal no longer matters to the athlete. Instead of trying to manufacture motivation out of thin air, they can either find a different goal or take a break from active goal pursuit.

It is difficult to fix a problem that hasn't been correctly defined. For this reason, an important early step in the process of helping an athlete make the best of a bad situation is getting them to articulate their understanding of the problem. This is useful even when your understanding of the problem matches the athlete's description of it, but it has all the more value when it doesn't. At this point, you have the opportunity to talk through the different possibilities with the athlete and come to an agreement.

Be careful not to push athletes toward your understanding of the problem. Instead of giving them your theory, ask them a question that presents one or more possibilities beyond their own assessment. Motivational interviewing is grounded in the insight that people are more likely to change their minds about something when they change their own mind instead of having change forced on them by someone else. That's why it's called motivational interviewing and not motivational lecturing.

Returning to the example of loss of motivation, after hearing the athlete say they don't know what's wrong with them and they need to get their motivation back, you might ask, "Have you considered the possibility that you've simply lost interest in your goal, and if you let go of feeling obligated to remain motivated by it, the problem will disappear?" At this point it's really up to the athlete. You've given them a clear second option to consider alongside what they'd previously assumed was their only option. Whichever path they choose is likely to be the right one for them. If they decide their goal does in fact still matter to them, you can help them brainstorm ways to restore their motivation. If they decide they have truly lost interest in the goal, you can offer them another choice between taking a break from active goal pursuit and coming up with an alternative goal.

Try to get the athlete to clearly articulate what they want.

One thing to keep in mind when working through problems with athletes is that there is no separation between the athlete self and the broader self. People have only one mind; the mind they use to cope with life in general is the mind they also use to cope with sports-related challenges. For this reason, what seem like sports-related challenges oftentimes aren't really sports-related at their roots.

Take performance anxiety. At a superficial level, the common problem of experiencing intense fear of failure before races is just that: fear of failure. But if you were to explore where performance anxiety comes from in a certain athlete, you might discover that it's rooted in perfectionism associated with low self-esteem stemming from repeated parental criticism during childhood. Indeed, studies on performance anxiety in athletes have found that it commonly stems from this very source. For such an athlete, solving the problem of performance anxiety is likely to require that they address their perfectionistic tendencies and, to some extent, their low self-esteem.

We can all agree that it is difficult to fix a problem that has not been correctly defined. When the problem an athlete faces goes deeper than sport, correctly defining it will require that athlete and coach explore the problem's psychological underpinnings. In the case of performance anxiety, you can initiate this process simply by asking the athlete *why* they think they experience intense fear of failure before competing. Once it's on the table that this fear is rooted in perfectionism and low self-esteem, you and the athlete are empowered to find ways to use the training process to build the athlete's self-esteem and soften their perfectionistic tendencies so they're less afraid of failure on race day. If your exploration of potential solutions had remained focused on sports alone, you might never have made headway in addressing the issue.

Any sports-related problem that causes an athlete to experience strong negative emotions such as fear or anger presents an opportunity for the athlete to reflect on and express what they really want—who they want to be and what they value. An athlete who becomes paralyzed by fear of failure before races doesn't just want to overcome performance anxiety. They want to have a solid sense of self-worth that is impervious to failure. As a coach, you will have more success in helping athletes overcome a variety of challenges if you get them to talk openly about what they want for themselves both on an athletic level and on a human level.

Clearly articulate what you want for the athlete.

Athletes benefit from knowing what their coach wants for them when facing challenges. It makes them feel supported and helps them gain clarity on what they want for themselves. At the broadest level, what every coach should want for their athletes is overall well-being and satisfaction with their sport. These desires might seem too obvious to bear mentioning, but it's worthwhile to remind athletes that you have their best interests at heart whenever challenges arise.

Another thing that coaches should want for athletes is mental fitness, or the ability to make the best of the bad situations they encounter by fully accepting, embracing, and addressing them. Athletes who exhibit exceptional mental fitness in this way can be described as ***ultrarealists***. When one of your athletes suffers a setback, think about how an ultrarealist would handle it and then describe this ideal response to them. Make it clear that you do not necessarily expect them to successfully emulate it. You're merely presenting it as something for the athlete to aspire to.

Suppose a triathlete you're coaching suffers a pectoral muscle tear during a swim workout. A sports medicine specialist tells the athlete that the injury will take two weeks to heal, which is bad news because the athlete has an "A" race in six weeks. Most athletes in this situation will feel any number of negative emotions—disappointment, frustration, bitterness, anger, despair. Ultrarealists will feel these emotions as well, but instead of dwelling on them, they will quickly accept the reality of the setback and pivot from focusing on the problem to focusing on making the best of it. In Chapter 6, you will recall, we discussed the strategy of incremental retreat, which entails modifying training both as little and as much as necessary to attenuate the risk of a bigger breakdown when an injury has occurred. In the situation described, an ultrarealist is likely to practice incremental retreat by doing what they can in the pool—kick sets, drills that don't involve using the injured muscle, perhaps even one-armed swimming—instead of giving in to a "What's the point?" attitude and avoiding the water altogether for two weeks.

An ultrarealist will also look for a silver lining in the situation, embracing it as an opportunity to strengthen a weak flutter kick, or learn to breathe on their weak side, or make progress in some other area where progress was needed. Whereas a more typical athlete will become demoralized by their injury, assuming it puts their race goal out of reach, the ultrarealist will assume nothing. They will derive genuine satisfaction from completing the race knowing they made the very best of their misfortune, even if they don't achieve their original goal.

As godlike as this response to a poorly timed injury may seem, there are real, flesh-and-blood athletes in the world who are fully capable of it. You should want nothing less for your athletes in such situations, and you can help them move toward an ultrarealist mindset by clearly communicating this desire. Just take care to do it in a way that inspires them instead of making them feel inferior.

Let the athlete know that you aren't judging them and that the truth is always okay.

Oftentimes, accepting reality requires a person to acknowledge an unpleasant truth about themselves. A natural human instinct is to protect ourselves from unflattering self-knowledge. It inclines us toward using various forms of denial as a shield against reality. For example, athletes who are prone to overtrain commonly resist accepting the reality that pushing too hard is the true cause of consequences such as injury and fitness stagnation. Research has shown that certain psychological characteristics predispose athletes to overtrain. In some athletes this tendency is a manifestation of insecurity—a misguided effort to gain the confidence they lack. In others it expresses a kind of intellectual laziness—a desire for success to be as simple as outworking everyone else, when of course it isn't. People don't want to see themselves as insecure or mentally lazy, however, and for this reason, it can be difficult to get an athlete who tends to work too hard to admit they're doing so, and why.

There's a lot that you can do as a coach to help athletes overcome their fear of accepting uncomfortable realities. A poorly executed motivational interview can make the interviewee feel as if they are on trial. Be conscious of this risk in framing your questions and responses, especially on occasions when you are trying to get the athlete to see something about themselves that they don't see yet. For example, instead of asking, "Do you think that insecurity might be driving you to overtrain?" ask, "Do you have any ideas about why you find it difficult to trust that not pushing so hard in training might be beneficial for you?" It takes a bit longer for the truth to come to light with this approach, but the athlete is likely to be more receptive to it when it does.

There's no harm in being overt in expressing your intentions in these moments. Come right out and tell the athlete that you will never judge them for any of their foibles. Assure them that you are looking to unearth the real root of their self-limiting behaviors not because you wish to shame them but because it points the way to solutions.

Share facts and information with the athlete as needed to guide them toward a clearer picture of reality.

Suppose you're coaching an athlete who worries that they have the wrong body type for their sport—they are too tall, too short, too heavy, or too light to achieve their ambitions. One way to address this worry is to cite examples of athletes who have succeeded at the highest level of their sport despite having a body type outside the norm. If the athlete happens to be a rower who worries they're too small, you might tell them about Nathan Cohen and Joseph Sullivan, who won the men's double scull event for New Zealand at the 2012 Olympics despite being the two smallest competitors in the 15-team field.

In this type of situation, it's also helpful to cite examples of athletes who got themselves into trouble by worrying too much about their body type. There are plenty of elite athletes who achieved their ambitions only after learning to let go and focus on making the best of what they had. One notable athlete of this sort is Flora Duffy, a Bermudan triathlete whose career was derailed by an eating disorder and depression resulting from concerns about her weight. Fortunately, she rebounded to win three world championship titles and an Olympic gold medal after taking a break and shifting her focus back to simply enjoying her sport.

Coaches can use carefully chosen examples to correct an athlete's distorted view of reality—in this case, the distorted belief that one has to look a certain way to be successful in a sport, and that efforts to make one's body look more ideal for their sport automatically lead to better performance. Be careful how you deliver such correctives, though. If you're not sufficiently tactful, the athlete will hear only "You're wrong" and become defensive. Like other motivational interviewing techniques, this one should be used to guide athletes toward their own discoveries, not to tell them what's what.

This technique can be especially useful in diffusing shame in athletes who are unknowingly sabotaging themselves mentally in one way or another. It's a way to make the discussion about someone else (e.g., Flora Duffy) for the moment, giving them space to recognize themselves in another athlete's struggles.

When appropriate, use words like "normal" and "common" to reduce shame or self-judgment in the athlete.

Another way to diffuse potential shame in athletes who are holding themselves back mentally is to let them know that they are not alone in avoiding difficult topics or self-reflection. The truth is on your side here. The vast majority of mental limiters you will encounter in the athletes you coach—including performance anxiety, low motivation, self-doubt, and body dissatisfaction—are both normal and common. People take comfort in knowing they are not alone in their mental challenges. By making it clear to your athletes that they are not unique in their particular challenges, you will increase their readiness to accept, embrace, and address them.

Don't overpromise final outcomes. Focus on progress.

Again, developing mental fitness is a slow process. Athletes need to know and accept this reality as well, lest they become frustrated or demoralized by failure to meet unreasonable expectations for progress. Identifying a problem is only the first step toward solving it. The "aha" moment athletes experience when they come to accept that there is something they need to work on is not a substitute for the work itself. In the excitement of these important moments athletes often mistakenly assume they're one small step away from putting the problem behind them once and for all, which inevitably leads to disappointment.

Many of the self-limiting behaviors athletes engage in are rooted in the elements of their psychology that resist change. One example is catastrophizing, which is a tendency to see problems as being more significant than they really are. For athletes with this tendency, every niggle is a major injury, every bad workout a sign of declining fitness. Catastrophizing is often rooted in a lack of self-efficacy stemming from chaotic childhood environments. Getting an athlete to recognize this tendency and its consequences is a good first step, but neither you nor the athlete should expect an overnight resolution.

In these scenarios, it's helpful to remind athletes that progress is progress. Every bit of improvement they earn in the process of working on a self-limiting tendency, such as catastrophizing, will pay dividends in the forms of better outcomes after setbacks and a more enjoyable experience of the sport. It's okay to have a vision of what perfect handling of each setback looks like ("What would an ultrarealist do?"), but the focus should be on how far the athlete has come, not how far they have to go.

Be willing to challenge the athlete when you believe that doing so is in their best interest.

There are times when coaches need to challenge their athletes, not just physically but also mentally. All athletes have either a tacit or explicit image of the person they wish to be in practicing their sport. In other words, they have either an unconscious or conscious desire to train and compete as the best version of themselves. An important part of coaching the mind is helping athletes define who they want to be and what it means to train and race as the best version of themselves, and then challenge them to reach for this standard in key moments. It's important, however, that this ideal image come entirely from the athlete, not you. Challenge them gently and allow them to move forward at their own pace.

Imagine you're coaching an athlete who is prone to unhelpful comparisons. When they're just returning to training after an injury hiatus, they dwell on how unfit they are compared to before they got hurt. When they win their age group in a race, they lament how much faster they were ten years ago. This athlete needs to snap out of it and, as their coach, you can help them do so. Motivational interviewing can help here too.

You might start the process by asking the athlete if they believe that catastrophizing benefits them in any way. The obvious answer is no. Next, ask them if they believe there are athletes who manage to avoid catastrophizing the problems they face. The correct answer here is yes, but if the athlete needs proof, go ahead and offer an example or two. *The Comeback Quotient* tells the story of one such athlete, Geoffrey Kamworor, a Kenyan runner who fell at the start of the 2016 World Half Marathon Championship and was trampled by dozens of runners. Instead of panicking, he got up, chased down the lead group, and ultimately surged ahead to win the race. Ask the athlete if they admire how Kamworor chose to handle that moment and whether they would be proud to respond similarly to their own setbacks. If they answer yes, ask them if they are willing to try.

This is a challenging question, as the athlete can't refuse the invitation without essentially admitting that they are not willing to make an effort to be the athlete they claim to want to be. Again, though, these challenges must be presented gently, lest the athlete feel pushed. For example, you might propose a first step in which they simply acknowledge moments when they are catastrophizing. The goal of this step is not to change the unhelpful behavior but merely to create an in-the-moment awareness of it. Once the athlete is able to consistently acknowledge, "Here I go again," they will be in a much better position to alter their course. At first, they might only be able to channel their inner Geoffrey Kamworor amid small problems. With your continued support, they will stay calm during bigger and bigger setbacks, becoming more and more like the best version of themselves.

————————

We hope these examples of how to implement motivational interviewing in your coaching provide you with a good understanding of how mental fitness can be developed within the normal problem-solving process that is central to the athlete-coach relationship. Inasmuch as you help an athlete accept, embrace, and commit to making the best of the bad situations they encounter, that athlete will be forever changed, if only slightly. When the next problem occurs, the athlete will be a little more willing and able to accept, embrace, and commit to making the best of *that* particular situation, which is to say the athlete will demonstrate greater mental fitness.

Training for Mastery

There is a sense in which coaching the mind is the ultimate purpose of the endurance coach. At the beginning of this book, we stated that the job of a coach is to help athletes achieve their goals. Almost always, the goals athletes choose are symbols of improvement. They might not think of them as such, but that's what they really are. When an athlete sets their sights on a goal such as being the third to score on their cross country team or completing an Ironman 70.3 in less than 5 hours, it's not because these numbers have any intrinsic meaning or specialness. It's because these numbers represent improvement for them at this point in their athletic journey. That's why the athlete replaces these goals with new ones as soon as they've been achieved. The numbers lose all meaning when they no longer symbolize improvement.

Where does improvement lead ultimately? Sooner or later, every athlete comes to a point in their journey where the numbers stop getting better. But does this mean the athlete stops getting better at their sport? Not necessarily. Athletes may continue to gain knowledge of their sport and discover new ways to train smarter and compete more expertly long after they've set their last personal best. This deeper kind of improvement is called mastery, and it is the greatest goal that any athlete can aim for.

Mastery can be defined as justified confidence in one's ability to make the right decision whenever there is a decision to be made. Of course, no athlete makes the right decision in every situation. This is precisely why this deeper kind of improvement is always possible, a continuous ascent toward absolute decision-making confidence. As such, mastery is fundamentally a learning process, but a learning process in the fullest sense. Acquiring knowledge is only one part of it. To master a sport is also to become more observant, to hone instincts, to discover underlying principles, to gain wisdom, and to glean understanding from experience. Mastery is something an athlete can feel growing inside them—that's the confidence piece—and it feels terrific.

The journey toward mastery happens entirely in the mind. The body merely follows along, adapting to the mind's decisions. Each athlete's body has its own physical limits that are influenced by talent, fitness, and age. Mastery determines just how close to these limits the individual athlete is able to get. It is not at all uncommon for less talented, less fit, and older athletes to get closer to their physical limits by dint of greater mastery of their sport.

It is in this sense that the coach's ultimate function is to coach the mind. No matter what your athletes' immediate goals are, these goals are properly regarded as waypoints in an ongoing process of learning to master the sport. Understanding your role in this way has important implications for how you practice it. What you're really trying to do is give your athletes the ability to confidently make more and more good decisions in their training and racing. This doesn't necessarily mean you force them to design their own training schedules as soon as they are able to do so with competence. There are coaches who sometimes pass drink bottles to their athletes during workouts, and it's not because the athletes couldn't handle their own fueling logistics. There is something to be said for shouldering certain burdens for your athletes so they can focus on what's most important. But even to the extent that you continue to make decisions for your athletes, your overarching mission is to nudge them along toward being able to confidently make the right decision on their own whenever a decision is required. It could be a small one, such as whether to react to or ignore a competitor's surge during a race, or a big one, such as whether to shut down a macrocycle early due to nonfunctional overreaching or instead make a smaller adjustment.

The most important difference between individual improvement goals and the all-encompassing goal of pursuing mastery is that the former are outcome-focused, whereas the latter is process-focused. If you and your athletes consciously view it as your highest goal to attain mastery, then not a day will pass without an opportunity to enjoy the satisfaction of goal achievement, because mastery is learning and learning is constant, at least in the right conditions. Whenever you discuss a workout with an athlete—or just about anything else related to training and racing, for that matter—you should always do so with the aim of teasing out any lessons it might offer. Don't force it. Put on your motivational interviewer's hat and, instead of steering the conversation toward the teaching you have in mind, gently maneuver it in a way that gets the athlete to reflect on the experience under discussion, creating space for whatever lessons it might contain to emerge.

Coaching the mind effectively is not a matter of knowing all the answers, but of knowing how to manage a process that guarantees answers will eventually be found. It's a skill that requires a sophisticated approach to communicating with athletes, and few coaches are good at this on day one. Coaching is a learning process as well, and like the athletic process, it is never fully mastered. But even a relatively inexperienced coach can do a good job of building mental fitness in athletes by using the core principles of mental fitness development as a compass. Whenever a problem of any kind arises in an athlete's training or racing, your function is to help that athlete fully face the reality of the situation by accepting it, embracing it, and addressing it. It's that simple.

The Ethics of Coaching

↗ The asymmetrical power dynamic inherent in coach-athlete relationships makes it vitally important that coaches maintain high ethical standards in their role.

↗ It is not enough for coaches to have a general intention to do right and avoid doing wrong. A coach is far more likely to fulfill these intentions by adhering to the five principles of the 80/20 Endurance coaching code of ethics: humility, honesty, integrity, respect, and caring.

↗ Like the core principles of endurance training, the ethical principles of coaching act as a litmus test to apply when making decisions that affect athletes. Maintaining an ethical coaching practice is arguably more important than technical knowledge.

Coaching is an awesome responsibility. As a coach, you have tremendous influence over the athletes you work with. They trust you. If you tell them to do something, they will almost certainly do it. If you tell them something is true, they will probably believe you. Your words affect them. They care what you think about them and they want to please you.

Unlike friendships, the coach-athlete relationship is asymmetrical. In other words, coaches and athletes do not occupy interchangeable roles in relation to one another. The power dynamic is more complex, with the athlete often having the power to hire and fire the coach and the coach calling most of the shots from day to day. This is neither a good thing nor a bad thing, intrinsically, but good and bad things can be done with the power that coaches have vis-á-vis athletes. How many times has your news feed informed you of another scandal involving a coach who's done bad things with their power? How many movies have you seen about a (fictional or historical) coach who did good things with their power?

We are confident that *you* want to do only good things as a coach. Succeeding in this aim will require not only that you are competent in your role, but that you adhere to a strict code of ethics in performing it. You must possess a clear understanding of the difference between right and wrong and always choose what's right. The objective of this chapter is to present a basic code of ethics for you to adhere to in your coaching. This code is based on five core principles: humility, honesty, integrity, respect, and caring. We will address each of these principles and then conclude with a thought experiment designed to drive home the value of maintaining high ethical standards as a coach.

Humility

It's no accident that humility stands as the first principle in the 80/20 Endurance coaching code of ethics. Coaches are servants. The very nature of the role demands that those who occupy it put their athletes' interests first, which is an act of humility. This doesn't mean that ego-driven individuals can't be effective coaches. It just means that ego-driven individuals can't be ego-driven when functioning as coaches. The desire to be recognized and appreciated is a natural human trait and a strong motivator for many people. Possessing this trait doesn't disqualify you from coaching effectively. It's okay if you want to be *seen* as a good coach and not just *be* a good coach. But this desire should never influence any decision you make in your work. Focus exclusively on your athletes' success, not yours, and trust that your work won't go unappreciated or unnoticed.

Acting with humility on a consistent basis is not easy. It requires that you consciously guard against allowing your ego to control how you present yourself to athletes. Your ego wants your athletes to see you as better than you really are—to project a whitewashed version of you that is smarter, wiser, and more knowledgeable than the real you. Don't deny it—it's part of what makes you human. To coach with humility, you must suppress your ego-driven desire to maintain this illusion and allow your athletes to see the real you.

Let's look at an example. Suppose an athlete is talking to you about how different sports nutrition products affect them during training. In doing so, they use terms like "glucagon" and "reactive hypoglycemia" that you don't understand. It is evident, however, that the athlete assumes you *are*, in fact, familiar with these terms. Many coaches in this situation will instinctively stay quiet in an effort to preserve the illusion that they are knowledgeable of the topic being discussed. But this is not the most ethical course of action. It's better to let the athlete know they've gone deeper into the metabolic weeds than you ever have. You might even congratulate the athlete on their knowledge and ask them to share resources that will help you come up to speed on the topic so you can do a better job of guiding others in this area.

The reason many (perhaps even most) coaches won't admit ignorance is that they fear losing the athlete's respect. What's ironic about this fear is that the opposite happens when a coach admits they don't know something. It takes confidence for a coach to make such an admission, and athletes recognize this. When you resist the natural human temptation to hide your limitations from an athlete, they see confidence, and confidence commands respect. One of the simplest ways you can cultivate humility as a coach is to be willing to say, "I don't know," when it's the truest answer to a question you've been asked by an athlete.

Another way you can show humility—and the confidence that underlies humility—is by not criticizing other coaches in front of your athletes. Bashing other practitioners of one's craft is common in most professions, coaching included. It's really nothing more than a backdoor way of thumping one's own chest, and it reflects poorly on you. If you simply must boast, boast openly, shouting from the rooftops about how awesome you are. Don't compound the sin by trying to disguise your boasting by raging about how terrible other coaches are. If you routinely hesitate to offer criticism in situations where most coaches would take the bait, your athletes will notice, and they'll respect it. The most ethical and effective way to demonstrate to athletes that you are a superior coach is to *not* try to demonstrate to athletes that you are a superior coach, either directly or indirectly.

We want to make it clear that we're not preaching false modesty or meekness here. You shouldn't downplay your strengths any more than you hide your weaknesses. Keep in mind that athletes often choose coaches they look up to in one way or another. Your personal successes can serve as a valuable source of inspiration for your athletes. An athlete might want to work with you because of your own racing accomplishments or because of the success you've had with other athletes. If this is the case, then sharing your achievements, when appropriate, might improve your chances of succeeding with that athlete. Just be honest with yourself about your motivation for this type of sharing and try to talk about yourself only when it serves a clear and positive purpose for the athlete.

Honesty

As we've just seen, it takes a certain amount of honesty to practice humility, but honesty is a distinct principle that coaches must adhere to quite apart from its relationship to humility. Like any healthy relationship, a healthy coach-athlete relationship is built on trust, and trust is inspired by honesty. The more your athletes trust you, the more receptive they will be to your coaching, and the more honest you are with them, the more they will trust you.

It's never too soon to demonstrate honesty in your relationship with an athlete. In fact, you should start before you even meet them by being open and honest about the type of coach you are in your public messaging. Not every coach is a great fit for every athlete. Your particular style of coaching will resonate with some athletes more than others. Prospective clients should understand your approach to coaching before they make the decision to hire you. Articulate your way of coaching in clear terms on your website and in your initial consultation with each prospective client. For example, if you work best with highly motivated athletes and lose interest in those who don't consistently make their training a high priority, put it out there. By doing so, you will filter out athletes who aren't a good match for you while also inspiring trust in those who find your style appealing and appreciate the honesty you demonstrate in not pretending to be all things to all athletes.

Honesty is a two-way street, of course. No coach can succeed with an athlete who isn't honest with them. Some athletes are more honest by nature than others are, but most are capable of being honest with a coach who's honest with them. That's another reason to go out of your way to be candid with athletes from the beginning—not only are you eliciting their trust, but you're also making them feel comfortable with being just as open in return.

Everyone lies occasionally, including coaches. We're not going to tell you to never bend the truth with your athletes. It's a nice standard to aspire to, but also unrealistic. A more achievable standard, which all coaches should aspire to, is to bend the truth as little as possible in communicating with athletes, and only for the best of reasons. It's forgivable, for example, to say "I never doubted you!" to an athlete who did something you privately doubted they would do. But a coach should never lie to an athlete for lack of courage or out of sheer laziness. If you forget a meeting with an athlete, just admit it! Don't concoct some "my dog ate my homework" type of excuse. You will never regret being truthful in such situations. Much like humility, honesty exhibited when least expected has the opposite effect of what's feared. The reason you're reticent to admit a mistake is that you fear it will lower an athlete's opinion of you, but what it really does is make you stand out from other coaches (and other people) in a way that commands respect.

Understand that your athletes have the same fears you do. They will be tempted to lie or to withhold information from you to the precise extent they fear being judged for telling the truth. For this reason, it is important that you make athletes feel safe in telling you the truth, whatever it may be. This can be done in a few ways. One is to simply assure athletes that you will never pass judgment on them for anything they share with you. A single assurance of this sort probably won't do the trick, so be prepared to repeat it as often as necessary until the message has taken root. The more opportunistic you can be in timing the delivery of such assurances, the sooner they will be internalized by the athlete.

For example, suppose you teach an athlete one of your favorite mental tricks for deflating self-doubt during races. After the next race, you ask the athlete if the trick was helpful, and there's a slight hesitation on their side. This tips you off that they did not use the trick or they did use it and it didn't help, and they're now afraid to tell you. This is a great time to assure the athlete that it's okay if, in fact, they didn't use the trick or didn't find it helpful—you just want to know why, so you can give them a different tool to try in the next race.

You can reinforce this type of messaging by rewarding athletes for telling you uncomfortable truths. Returning to the previous example, imagine the athlete does admit to not finding your mental trick helpful, but is visibly uneasy in doing so. The right move here is to thank the athlete for being honest and congratulate them on having the courage to tell the truth. Then you can move on to discuss why and what to do about it.

Perhaps the most powerful way to make athletes feel comfortable in being fully truthful with you is modeling truthfulness in your interactions with them. Let's say you copy a workout from one athlete's training calendar to another's, but you neglect to convert the distances from metric units (which the first athlete uses) to English units for the second athlete. When the second athlete points out the error, you might be tempted to play it off as intentional, or at least to hide the true origin of the error. It's better, however, to simply apologize for the oversight, explain exactly what happened, and admit that you duplicate workouts all the time for efficiency's sake. If you're so inclined, assure the athlete that efficiency does not equal laziness and that you are giving your very best effort in planning their training, despite the occasional shortcut.

In the most successful coach-athlete relationships there is very little awkwardness or embarrassment felt or expressed on either side. If you can cultivate a zero-awkwardness atmosphere with an athlete, you have done something praiseworthy. Faithful adherence to the principle of honesty will go a long way toward creating this healthy atmosphere.

Integrity

Integrity is often thought of as being synonymous with honesty, but in the 80/20 Endurance coaching code of ethics it has a distinct meaning. Simply put, integrity is doing what you say you'll do. If your words and your deeds align, you have integrity. If they don't, you're a hypocrite.

In coaching, integrity begins with competence. Athletes tend to assume that coaches know what they're doing. The principle of integrity requires that you be as competent as athletes assume you are. In other words, integrity demands that you be the best coach you can possibly be. In turn, being the best coach you can be demands that you continually strive to be better. To this end, carve out some time every day to work on expanding your knowledge and developing your skillset. Stay current on relevant research, learn about other coaches, and plug holes in your repertoire (for example, by taking a deep dive into biomechanics). High-integrity coaches never become complacent. They always believe they can improve and continuously take active measures to hone their craft.

Growing as a coach also means growing as a person. All coaches have weaknesses. Part of being the best coach you can be is identifying and addressing your weaknesses as a coach. Some weaknesses are superficial. Perhaps you don't know enough about running shoes to ensure that footwear issues don't interfere with your runners' success. That's an easy fix. Other weaknesses are not superficial and addressing them is as much a matter of personal growth as it is a matter of professional growth. There might be a certain type of athlete you struggle to connect with—older athletes, younger athletes, male athletes, female athletes, knowledgeable athletes, not-so-knowledgeable athletes, etc. What does that say about you? We'll tell you: It says you can do better!

Integrity has a commercial dimension that is also worthy of consideration. Either directly or indirectly, most athletes pay for their coaches' services. In business, integrity is demonstrated by giving customers their money's worth. Coaching is like any other enterprise in this regard. It's a good idea to ask yourself—not just once, but routinely— *Am I giving my athletes their money's worth?* Most times, you will be. But if you're honest with yourself, you will have to admit that, on occasion, you're not. There's a natural tendency among coaches to get a bit complacent with athletes they've been working with for a long time. Are you giving as much time and energy to the athlete you've coached for two years as you are to the athlete you've been coaching for two weeks? If not, do something about it.

In your efforts to give athletes their money's worth, it's helpful to clearly define the value you're offering in return for payment. A simple list that includes both hard and soft responsibilities can serve this function. Hard responsibilities are concrete deliverables that are explicitly agreed upon by coaches and athletes. An example of a hard responsibility is updating each athlete's training schedule once a week. Failure to meet such responsibilities is the exact equivalent of a service lapse in another profession, such as a waiter forgetting to serve a diner's salad dressing on the side. Soft responsibilities are your own private standards. For example, one of your soft responsibilities might be to check the weather forecast in each athlete's location before you go to bed, just in case conditions are not conducive to the next day's scheduled training. Private rules like this one give you something concrete to use in assessing whether you are delivering full value to your athletes.

It should be said that all of the integrity guidelines we've given you are intended to ensure fairness not just to your athletes but also to you, the coach. There are athletes out there who, unfortunately, will take advantage of their coach if allowed to. Having a list of hard responsibilities can prevent you from being taken advantage of. Many coaches offer different tiers of service. An athlete at the lowest tier of service cannot expect to receive as much of your time and energy as an athlete at the highest tier, but this doesn't mean some athletes might not try to see what they can get away with. In these cases, the specific deliverables that you and the athlete have agreed upon give you a basis for holding a firm line. You can even tell an overly demanding athlete that, as much as you might like to do A, B, or C for them, you must refrain out of fairness to the athletes who pay for these services.

There are other ways in which the words you speak and the things you do must align, if you are to call yourself a coach of integrity. We can't cover them all, but one that mustn't go unmentioned is confidentiality. For better or worse, coaching is much less tightly regulated than many other professions, including medicine. The kinds of strict privacy laws that protect patients don't exist in coaching, yet the expectations are the same, and they should be. In many successful coach-athlete relationships, the athlete shares a lot of personal information with their coach, and they don't intend for you to pass it along to anyone else. If you wish to share a bit of personal information an athlete has disclosed to you—perhaps because you believe it will help another athlete—ask permission first. Some athletes give their coaches blanket permission to share, and that's fine. The thing you're trying to avoid, even with these "open book" types, is saying or doing anything you wouldn't want the athlete to know you're saying or doing. It's easy to let your words and your actions slip out of alignment when you know that no one will be the wiser, but true integrity means your words and actions align even when the risk of exposure is minimal.

Respect

The first three principles in the 80/20 Endurance code of coaching ethics—humility, honesty, and integrity—are ways of conducting oneself. The last two—respect and caring—are ways of *feeling*, in addition to being ways of conducting oneself. Does this mean we're telling you how you should feel? Not exactly. It is not our place to try to control your heart. But we will say that anybody who is incapable of genuinely respecting and caring about individual athletes should not be a coach. Nor should you coach any individual athlete you don't respect or care about.

To respect others is to both regard them and treat them as your equals. Only genuine respect counts as respect. Treating others as your equals is better than not doing so, but it's better still to feel in your heart that others are your equals. When you do this, respectful treatment becomes almost automatic. No athlete you coach should ever have to earn your respect. You should respect each athlete implicitly from the moment you first meet them. We can't stop you from losing respect for athletes who exhibit a lack of character, and we'll say more about that in a moment. But until and unless they demonstrate otherwise, all athletes, without exception, should be assumed to be worthy of your respect.

When we say "all athletes," we mean just that: all ages, all sexes and sexual orientations, all races and ethnicities, all nationalities, all religions, all levels of education and wealth, all professions, all political persuasions, and all personality types. If you're like most people, you are slower to respect and quicker to disrespect certain types of people, perhaps unconsciously. To be a coach of integrity, you need to identify and eradicate any such biases that exist in you. As you go through life, notice when you feel a lack of respect for particular people, and look for patterns. Are there certain types of people you hold to a higher standard than others? If so, recognize that this is unacceptable and work hard to overcome your bias, whatever it may be.

The one acceptable reason for losing respect for an athlete is, as suggested above, behavior that shows a lack of character. Not every athlete is worthy of your coaching. If an athlete is abusive toward you, lies egregiously or willfully withholds important information from you, violates the rules of fair play, or misbehaves in any other way that causes you to lose respect for them, you have every right to terminate the relationship. In fact, you have a duty to terminate the relationship. In summary, if your lack of respect for a given athlete is on you, work to improve, and if your lack of respect for an athlete is on them, let them go—respectfully.

Caring

The fifth and final principle of the 80/20 Endurance coaching code of ethics—caring—is the least teachable. In fact, it's completely unteachable. Caring comes from within. You cannot care about the athletes you coach merely because a textbook on coaching said you should. Either you care about them or you don't. And if you don't, then coaching is the wrong profession for you. As the legendary American football coach Bobby Dodd put it, "Either love your players or get out of coaching."

There are, however, right and wrong ways to care about the athletes you coach, and this part can be taught. Let's first describe the right way to care about your athletes. An ethical coach cares more about their athletes as human beings than they care about them as athletes. If there should ever arise a situation where you believe that a potential athletic success will come at an unacceptable cost to an athlete's physical or mental well-being, it becomes your ethical responsibility to stand in the way of that potential success.

Coach-athlete partnerships are more personal than other transactional relationships, such as those between doctors and patients. Patients typically see their doctor only when they need to, whereas many athletes have daily contact with their coach. Over time, coaches and athletes get to know each other well and may establish a close bond. It is not uncommon for athletes to develop a deep affection for, and a strong attachment to, their coach. We've all heard professional athletes gush about their coach in interviews after a big victory. There is a lot riding on this relationship for many athletes, and when a coach comes through for them, their gratitude is immense. Mutual caring between a coach and an athlete can be a major factor in the athlete's success. The familiar trope of the athlete who will run through a wall for their coach has a solid foundation in reality. When you care about your athletes, they care about you in return, and you're able to get more out of them.

Caring can be expressed in many ways, and by any personality type. Some coaches have nurturing personalities and express caring in a nurturing way. Others have brusque personalities and express caring in a brusque way. Regardless of your personality type, just be yourself and express caring in a way that's natural for you. When you care, you care, and athletes know it.

Never lose sight of the fact that the coach-athlete relationship is a professional one. Your expressions of caring for the athletes you work with must never breach the bounds of professionalism. You are being paid to provide a service. The fact that you like or enjoy the company of a particular athlete doesn't change this reality. In psychotherapy there is a general prohibition against so-called dual relationships that should be respected in coaching as well. This means you cannot occupy two roles in relation to an athlete. You might see no harm in thinking of one or more athletes you coach as your friends, but this should be avoided because it blurs the boundaries of the relationship in ways that could lead to problems.

Suppose an athlete, whom you've allowed to see you as a friend, experiences money troubles and asks you to coach them for free for a period of time "out of friendship." There's nothing wrong with taking on the occasional pro bono client, but this should be done as a professional matter and not because you've allowed things to get too personal with an athlete. Another thing to keep in mind is that all coach-athlete relationships come to an end at some point, and these inevitable separations are a lot cleaner when the relationship doesn't have a dual nature.

Maintaining strict professionalism in your relationships with athletes is also important because of the power dynamics involved. A coach is in a position of authority. Even when the athlete is in control of hiring and firing, the coach is likely to have greater "soft power." For this reason, it is untenable for coaches and athletes to maintain a second, personal relationship with a different power dynamic. The obvious case is romantic involvement. For the same reason it is unethical for employers to have any kind of sexual relationship with employees, coaches must never cross this line with their athletes. Even if both parties in the relationship are unattached adults, such entanglements are marred by an unequal power balance that is unhealthy, not just in romantic relationships, but in nonsexual friendships too. A coach who develops romantic feelings for an athlete has an obligation to terminate the relationship, regardless of whether they wish to pursue a separate, personal relationship.

The principle of caring has a special application for coaches of youth athletes. Because youth athletes are not yet fully mature, their coaches are responsible for them in a way they are not for adult clients. Caring about youth athletes is above all a matter of protecting them from physical and emotional harm and playing a positive role in their growth and development. Compared to coaching adults, coaching children is less a matter of helping them achieve goals and more a matter of using sport as a vehicle for nurturing a passion for athletics and cultivating life skills. Youth sports coaches should have a good understanding of child psychology and of the developmental needs of children in the specific age bracket they're managing. Relevant resources are provided at the back of this book.

A THOUGHT EXPERIMENT

The TV show *Ted Lasso* is about an American college football coach who was hired to lead AFC Richmond, an English professional soccer team. Lasso knew nothing about soccer, which was precisely the point. The team's owner chose him in an effort to spite her ex-husband, who loved the team and was sure to be devastated if incompetent coaching caused it to flounder. But to the owner's dismay, Lasso overcame some initial fumbling to achieve great success with AFC Richmond.

Like all works of fiction, *Ted Lasso* is not completely realistic, but the events it depicts are not entirely fantastical either. Indeed, there are famous, factual examples of individuals who achieved tremendous success as coaches despite initially knowing little about the sport they coached. One is Brother Colm O'Connell, an Irish missionary who had no clue how to train distance runners when he was handed the job of coaching track and cross country at St. Patrick's High School in Iten, Kenya, yet his program went on to produce numerous world and Olympic champions and world-record breakers. That's because effective coaching is about much more than knowing the sport one coaches.

The preceding chapters of this book have focused on the knowledge side of coaching endurance sports. In the present chapter, we've shifted our attention to the interpersonal side of the job, which is just as important, perhaps more important.

What Ted Lasso lacked in soccer knowledge he made up for in coaching ethics. He succeeded with AFC Richmond because he coached his players with humility, honesty, integrity, respect, and caring. If, by comparing yourself against more knowledgeable coaches, you ever begin to doubt your value as a coach, call a timeout and conduct the following thought experiment: Pretend you know even less about the sport than you do. In fact, pretend that some weird kind of selective amnesia has caused you to forget everything you ever learned about it. Could you still coach it effectively? With enough humility, honesty, integrity, respect, and caring, you probably could.

The Business
of Coaching

⚊ There are three basic endurance coaching career models: the youth team/club model, the adult team/club model, and the remote/independent model. There are also a variety of niches within each model. Choosing the right model and niche for you will greatly increase your chances of succeeding as a coach.

⚊ It's important to take the long view in launching a coaching career. Expect it to begin with a period of dues-paying that includes building your résumé and reputation, networking, and leveraging smaller immediate opportunities to earn bigger future opportunities.

⚊ Coaches who choose to pursue the remote/independent model need to take time to get certain things in place—including creating a budget, getting insured, and creating a professional website—before launching a business.

⚊ Coaching services require a well-thought-out marketing strategy and consistent energy to back it up. There are many cost-effective or free ways to market a coaching business, such as adding a profile to online coach directories, posting high-quality coaching content on social media, and blogging.

P eople become endurance coaches because they're passionate about endurance sports and they enjoy helping athletes achieve their goals, not because they're money hungry. Nevertheless, a coach must earn a livable income through coaching if they wish to keep doing it. In this sense, coaching is a business like any other, and it must be approached as such.

A lot of coaches fail to survive in the profession not because they're bad at coaching but because they're bad at business. Taking the business side of coaching seriously will give you a competitive advantage in the marketplace. It may never be your favorite part of the job, but giving it your best effort could be the thing that enables you to do the part you do enjoy—coaching—for a long time to come.

There is more than one way to make a decent living as an endurance coach. In this chapter we will discuss three different models: the youth team/club model, the adult team/club model, and the remote/independent model. Because the greatest amount of opportunity exists in the last of these options, we'll spend the bulk of our time there, covering topics that include getting started, budgeting and billing, scheduling and time management, marketing and recruiting clients, and client retention and growth management.

Find Your Niche

An important and often overlooked element of success in endurance coaching is finding one's niche. There's more than one path a coach can take within any given coaching model. Those who find the most success are typically the ones who choose a path that is uniquely theirs, based on who they are, what they've experienced, and what they're most interested in. Too many aspiring coaches make the mistake of blindly following someone else's path or just fumbling along without ever really reflecting on what they want their niche to be. The more thought you put into choosing a direction that's right for you, the more likely it is that you'll still be coaching in five or ten years.

Consider what makes you different and special as a coach. Perhaps you're really good with younger or older athletes. Maybe you have a knack for helping injury-prone athletes or athletes with mental-health challenges. It could be that you're especially passionate about working with back-of-the-pack athletes or elite athletes. Or you might be uniquely strong as a motivator or a science geek. Whatever it is that makes you special as a coach, go with it. Don't look over your shoulder at what other coaches are doing. While it's important that you be guided by general best practices in your coaching work, doing things one's own way, to some extent, is itself a best practice in endurance coaching.

If you haven't yet reflected much on what kind of coach you are or want to be, start now by sitting down and writing out a description of your individual style, approach, or specialty. If it's too soon for this exercise to have much value, wait a bit. But don't wait forever, or else the path you wander down might not be the right one for you. The next three sections are intended to help you avoid this fate, supplying concrete guidelines for finding success on your terms in each of the three major endurance coaching models.

The School Team/Youth Club Model

Before the rise of the internet and the attending explosion in adult endurance sports participation, the vast majority of jobs available for endurance coaches existed within schools and youth clubs. These jobs still exist, but they've been overshadowed by internet-based remote coaching opportunities. If you enjoy working with younger athletes, prefer a team environment, and like the structure of school- or team-based coaching, the school team/youth club model might be the best fit for you.

It's not really a single model, however. Youth clubs, secondary/high school teams, and university teams are distinct, and it's rare for a coach to switch from one of these tracks to another. Employers in each environment tend to hire coaches with prior experience in the same environment, so it's best to choose one and go all in.

Studying the résumés of established coaches within your chosen track will give you a good idea of how to get started. Relevant certifications are required for employment in many schools and clubs and are almost always preferred, even when not strictly required. In the United States, for example, you'll probably need a USA Swimming certification to get a job coaching a youth swim club, while a USA Track & Field certification will improve your chances of getting a job coaching cross-country or track and field at a competitive high school, and a USA Triathlon certification is all but indispensable if you wish to lead a collegiate triathlon club.

Coaches who choose the youth team/youth club model often get their first bit of professional experience in assistant roles. The advantages of assistantships are that they are a lot easier to obtain than head coaching jobs, and they are excellent opportunities to build a résumé, hone your craft, and prove your ability. Their disadvantages are that they don't pay well and they don't always lead to swift advancement. However, there's another way to look at these disadvantages, which is that they tend to weed out coaches who aren't as passionate and determined as you. Success doesn't happen overnight in any profession. Coaches destined for success are willing to pay their dues.

Once you've gotten your foot in the door, take full advantage of the opportunity you've been awarded by giving it everything you've got. Be organized, punctual, and professional. Avoid the trap of automatically doing things the way they've always been done just because they've always been done that way. Instead, look for ways to do them better (without irking your boss if you work under a head coach!). Be energetic and enthusiastic, as if there's no other group you'd rather be coaching. Cultivate a sense of pride and tradition. For example, have a legendary former member of the team or club return to give a talk, order special team T-shirts emblazed with a youth-friendly slogan, or host an annual end-of-season barbecue. Make each member of the group feel like the most important member. Don't bide your time until you get where you want to be in your career—make the place you are now feel like the ultimate place to be, for you and for everyone around you.

The Adult Team/Club Model

Adult-focused endurance teams and clubs exist all over the world, with new ones being created all the time. Many of these clubs employ coaches. If you enjoy working in person with athletes, you prefer coaching adults over children, and you like the less-structured environment of an adult-focused club, then this model might be for you.

The first major fork you will encounter along this path is the choice between starting your own team or club or attaching yourself to an existing one. Each option has its pros and cons. The obvious advantage of attaching yourself to an existing entity is that the work of building it has already been done, so there's less risk involved. The biggest disadvantage is that you might need to wait in line before you take over as the group's top coach, and you might never have as much power to shape the culture as you would like. The pros and cons of starting your own team or club are just the reverse—more work, more risk, less waiting, and more control. The two options are not mutually exclusive, of course. You could start with an existing group, gain experience and confidence, and then strike out on your own.

Local networking is essential to launching a successful independent endurance sports group. If you were to start such a group next week, who would show up at the first workout? How would you make athletes aware of it? Endurance coaches who succeed in launching their own adult team or club are typically well-known and respected in their local athletic community. If you're not there yet, take some time to bootstrap your way there by getting involved in your local athlete community. Build relationships with race directors, store owners, and facility managers. Earn a reputation among local athletes as that person who always shows up. Be generous and helpful, so that others think well enough of you that, when the time comes, they're willing to participate in the first workout you host for your new team or club.

The true goal, naturally, is not merely to start or get a job with a team or club, but to help a group of athletes flourish and, in turn, to flourish as a coach. To achieve this goal, you must create and sustain a sense of community, an environment where every member feels involved in a substantive way. There are proven methods to do this. One is frequent contact. Schedule as many in-person meetups as you can create a demand for, and not just for workouts, but for social events as well (e.g., an Olympic Marathon watch party). Supplement these gatherings with online video chats, perhaps with interesting guest speakers. Start a team book club. Email an inspirational quote of the day to the full group. Collectively, such touchpoints create a social gravity that draws people in.

Another time-tested way to foster a sense of community is to empower individual members. In the most vibrant teams and clubs, the head coach is not the only leader. You want to encourage leadership within your group's ranks. Designate "captains" to lead different pace groups in workouts. Bestow assistant coaching responsibilities on an older member of the group who has a lot of wisdom to share. Sharing power benefits everyone in adult-level endurance sports teams and clubs.

You can further this effect by not just empowering but also recognizing individual members. Every athlete in a group—even the least competitive—wants to be recognized in one way or another. Give them that. Celebrate successes and milestones. Name an athlete of the month. Give birthday shout-outs. In the most flourishing adult teams and clubs, everyone gets their star turn, so to speak. It's not only good coaching, but it also inspires loyalty and commitment.

The Remote/Independent Model

The majority of adult endurance athletes who work with a coach do so remotely, through the internet. Coaches who choose this model are attracted by its flexibility and scalability. When you don't have to be physically present with athletes for workouts and races, you can coach more people in more places and do so on your own schedule. But it is these attractions that have drawn large numbers of coaches to remote/independent coaching, creating a competitive marketplace in which success does not come easily. Nevertheless, coaches who bring above-average levels of competence, professionalism, and hustle to the market succeed more often than not.

On a practical level, success in the remote/independent model relies on breaking through the noise (i.e., making athletes aware that you exist and would like to coach them) and delivering a first-class coaching experience. You want athletes to give you a try and then be glad that they did—so glad, in fact, that they sing your praises on social media and bring referrals to you!

INVEST IN YOUR BUSINESS

The first step is investing in yourself. Before you set up shop, take time to build a résumé that impresses. Strengthen your own athletic credentials, get certified, cultivate a social media following, and gain coaching experience where you can. Remember, you only get one chance to make a first impression. Do what it takes to ensure that athletes who are shopping for coaches take you seriously from the moment you open your doors for business.

In addition to building a résumé, you'll need to check some practical and logistical boxes before you formally launch your online coaching business. First among these is creating a website. Spend some time poking around the websites of other endurance coaches. Online coaching platforms such as TrainingPeaks make it easy to size up the competition. Note what you like and don't like about their design and layout, navigation, content, tools, and features. This will help you create a vision for your own site. Do you want to lead with athlete testimonials? Include a short inspirational video introducing yourself? Use some kind of interactive tool such as a free zone calculator to draw visitors in? There's no single right answer to any of these questions, but you will want to decide on what's right for you before you proceed.

If you are computer savvy and budget-conscious, you might want to consider building your own website. Platforms like WordPress make the DIY approach relatively painless. Just be aware that building your own website can be harder than expected for the inexperienced. The results don't always match the quality that a professional web designer can achieve. To find a professional web designer for your coaching website, ask for personal referrals from trusted sources, contact the designers of websites you especially like, or search through online freelancer databases such as Upwork.

ESTABLISH A BUSINESS STRUCTURE

Another important decision to be made is whether to go into business as an individual or create a legal business entity for your coaching work. In the U.S., many independent coaches choose to establish a limited liability corporation (LLC) for their coaching. These structures offer several advantages. One is that they create legal separation between your personal and business finances. For example, debt accumulated by the business cannot be treated as personal debt by debt collectors. There are also tax advantages associated with setting up an LLC, including the ability to treat business income as personal income. It's helpful, as well, to have an LLC in place if you plan to do any hiring in the future, as it minimizes your personal responsibility for these employees or contractors.

The disadvantages of incorporating are cost and paperwork, although neither factor is prohibitive for most coaches. In the U.S., the cost of creating an LLC ranges from $50 to $500, depending on which state you file in, and it usually takes a few weeks to receive state approval of an application. Online resources, such as LegalZoom, will walk you through the process step by step for a modest additional fee. Each country has its own system, of course, so be sure to base your decision on whether to create a separate entity for your coaching business on the specifics of your local system.

ACQUIRE INSURANCE PROTECTION

Insurance protection is something else you might want to have in place before you formally launch your coaching business. A basic liability coverage package will protect you financially if an athlete has an accident and tries to hold you legally responsible. Many endurance sport governing bodies offer liability insurance for coaches. You can further protect yourself by asking athletes to sign a liability waiver as part of your new client onboarding process. Hiring a lawyer to draft a waiver that is specific to your needs will give you the greatest protection, but there are standard templates online that you can adapt to serve the same function more affordably.

CREATE A BUDGET

Speaking of money, it's a good idea to create a budget for your coaching business prior to launch. How much money are you willing to spend to get your coaching career started, and on what? It doesn't need to be anything fancy. If you can make a household budget, you can make a budget for your coaching business that serves the purpose of preparing you for the necessary outlays. In the absence of such preparation, you'll have to make each spending decision independently without the security of a plan to reference it against. Here's a simple example of a coaching business startup budget:

Website	$500
Online coaching platform subscription	$50
Insurance	$100
Legal expenses	$500
	$1,150

Note that a launch budget is distinct from the accounting system you will use to manage your business finances once you're up and running. We recommend that you use one of the many accounting software solutions available to meet this need. Popular offerings include QuickBooks, Excel Bookkeeping, and Wave Accounting. These easy-to-use products will help you send invoices, make payments, track and manage expenses and revenues, pay taxes, and create budgets and forecasts. We recommend that you link your chosen accounting product or service with a business bank account and credit card that are used exclusively for your coaching work.

Define Your Services

There are three main categories of service that remote/independent endurance coaches offer athletes: one-on-one coaching, custom training plan design, and ready-made training plan sales. A fourth service, live training sessions, is more limited in its viability but deserving of mention. Most coaches center their business on individual coaching, so we will give it the greatest attention in this section, but let's first address the other options.

Live Training Sessions

A silver lining of the COVID-19 pandemic was that it forced endurance athletes to get resourceful in their efforts to stay fit. Deprived of in-person options for group training, many turned to iFit and other live training services delivered through the internet. A few enterprising endurance coaches took advantage of the demand for this type of service by hosting live workouts of their own. Demand for coached, live workouts has continued.

Indoor cycling workouts are most popular, but some endurance coaches have found success with running, strength, and mobility workouts as well. These sessions can be delivered in a variety of ways. The Zwift platform allows athletes to perform hosted virtual group rides in real time, while various smartphone apps provide video feeds enabling athletes to follow an instructor visually, and some coaches take a DIY approach using Facebook Live, Instagram live, and similar platforms.

It remains to be seen how many endurance coaches will be able to make live workout instruction a cornerstone of their business, but big players in the endurance coaching space, such as Purple Patch, are making a go of it. If this service plays to your strengths, consider making a go of it as well.

Ready-made Training Plans

A ready-made training plan is a plan created—usually online—for general use by athletes. Examples are "Beginner Marathon Plan" and "Level 3 Gravel Race Plan." There is a huge market for ready-made endurance training plans because athletes recognize the need for expert training guidance, but they aren't always willing or able to pay for individualized coaching. However, because these products are offered at a lower price point, they aren't a great revenue generator for coaches unless they are able to sell them in large numbers, and, with so many established coaches and coaching businesses offering ready-made plans, it is not easy to move them in bulk.

One of the keys to gaining traction with ready-made training plans is making them distinct from other plans in both substance and style. Your plans should have a specific appeal or meet a need that is not sufficiently met already in the marketplace. For example, you might build a special collection of triathlon training plans for athletes who hate swimming and play up this angle in your marketing and promotion of the plans.

Even if you don't intend to make ready-made training plan sales the cornerstone of your coaching business, consider at least making them a part of your overall strategy. Creating a suite of plans will give you a chance to define and refine your approach to the training process. Once the plans are built, they can serve as templates for more individualized offerings.

Some coaches use free ready-made plans as a "loss leader" that funnels athletes toward paid services. For example, you might give away a 12-week base-training plan and either insert a pitch for more sophisticated premium plans or for one-on-one coaching, or use email capture to follow up with users of the free plan after they've completed it. Another option is to resell 80/20 Endurance plans through our affiliate program. This allows you to make a little money off ready-made training plan sales without going through the effort to build plans, while still getting the opportunity to upsell.

Custom Training Plans

Underutilized by endurance coaches, custom training plans fill the gap between ready-made training plans and one-on-one coaching. They're a great option for athletes because unlike ready-made plans they are tailored to individual needs and preferences, yet they're more affordable than one-on-one coaching. At the same time, on a per-plan basis, they bring in more revenue for coaches than ready-made plans and they're more scalable than one-on-one coaching.

If you choose to offer this service, be sure to spell out the terms very clearly on your website. We recommend that you do not include ongoing monitoring of training or free adjustments to plans after delivery. These amenities make the service more time-intensive, less scalable, and also less differentiated from one-on-one coaching. Because custom plans vary greatly in length, your fee should be based on plan length. But payment for the full plan should be required either upfront or at the time it is delivered, regardless of its length.

Some coaches choose to deliver custom training plans in smaller blocks, four weeks being a typical block size. This approach has the advantage of allowing the coach to base each block on the results of the preceding one, better serving the athlete. The disadvantage is that it blurs the line between custom plan design and one-on-one coaching, causing some athletes to wonder why they should bother paying more for the latter.

To create truly customized training plans, you will of course need to gather all of the necessary information from athletes (see Appendix A). Feel free to use the custom training plan questionnaire available on the 80/20 Endurance website as a template for yours. A certain amount of back-and-forth may be required to fill in informational gaps, clarify unclear responses, and push back on unrealistic ideas from the athlete, which are common (that's why athletes need coaches!). For example, if an athlete says in the questionnaire that they plan to "sprinkle a few shorter races" into a custom marathon training plan you build for them, reply that you need to know exact dates and distances for any and all races they intend to do within the plan window before you can begin to build it. Races are highly disruptive to the training process and cannot be sensibly "sprinkled into" a plan that wasn't built around them.

Don't be afraid to turn away athletes whose requests don't align with your training philosophy or that constrain your ability to do your job properly. Suppose an athlete requests that you include thrice-weekly Orange Theory workouts (i.e., high-intensity group fitness classes) in the custom marathon training plan you build for them, something that would make it almost impossible for the plan to have an 80/20 intensity balance. In this case, explain to the athlete that asking a coach to create a training plan with other people's workouts is like asking a chef to cook a meal without having a say in the ingredients. It isn't always easy to turn away business, but you should never compromise your coaching standards for money's sake.

The custom training plan service is fundamentally intended to prepare athletes for their next "A" race. There has to be some end point to these plans, after all, and few other end points make much sense. As a coach, you have to know where athletes are going in order to chart the best path toward that destination. That being said, there are some cases where a custom plan can be built around a different goal, such as fat loss.

Also, it's a good idea to schedule calendar alerts reminding you when each client's "A" race is imminent so you can send them a note of encouragement a day or two before the event. This is not just good coaching but also good business, as the goodwill it engenders tends to transform first-time customers into repeat customers.

One-on-One Coaching

If you were the first person ever to offer one-on-one coaching services through the internet, you would have to figure out a lot of things for yourself. Lucky for you, thousands of online endurance coaches have come before you, and the model is well developed. However, there is flexibility within this model so let's review the key decisions that individual coaches need to make on pricing and billing, communication, workflow, and roster management.

Pricing and Billing

Monthly billing is the norm in online endurance coaching, and with good reason. Weekly billing would be a nuisance for both the coach and the athlete, and it would set the wrong expectation about the partnership, which will take months, not weeks, to bear real fruit. Quarterly or yearly billing, on the other hand, tends to make athletes feel locked in. Monthly billing cycles are also the norm in fitness clubs and online training platforms, hence familiar to athletes.

Monthly fees range broadly in online coaching, from as little as $100 per month to as much as $1,500 per month. Here are some factors to consider in deciding on your rates:

- **the specific sport or sports you coach**: Running coaches, for example, typically charge less than triathlon coaches.
- **your experience level**: Your rates should increase over time as you gain experience.
- **demand**: A coach with a full client roster and a waiting list can charge more than a coach struggling to fill their client roster.
- **the level of service you provide**: The more time you put into your athletes, the more you can charge.

Broadly speaking, aim to set your fees at a level that is fair to your clients, to you, and to the coaching profession. Undercutting the market with low pricing hurts everyone.

We recommend that you automate the billing process through PayPal, Stripe, or a similar service. Doing so not only eliminates any chance of forgetting to invoice athletes but also allows you to keep your personal interactions focused on things other than money. We recommend that you also avoid requiring any kind of long-term commitment from athletes. This practice demonstrates confidence in your ability to deliver results and minimizes perceived risk on the athlete's side. Although coach-athlete relationships are meant to be long-lasting, they don't always work out so it's best if both the coach and the athlete have the freedom to withdraw from the partnership at any time.

Communication

The actual work of coaching is done almost entirely through communication between coaches and athletes. Simply stated, without communication, there is no coaching. In the remote coaching model, communication options are limited, so coaches pursuing this model need to decide how they wish to communicate with athletes and create standards around these interactions. No single communication process is best for every coach, but the process you settle on must meet both your needs and the athlete's needs, and be appropriate in relation to your fees.

At a minimum, there should be some interaction around most or all of the completed workouts that athletes upload to their training log. Athletes should be encouraged to comment on how they experienced the workout, and coaches should, at the very least, acknowledge each completed workout and also answer questions, offer analysis, and give pointers as necessary. A great deal of useful coaching can be achieved through this channel alone, and some coaches prefer to make it the exclusive channel through which they interact with clients.

Audio or video consultations are not essential in the way that training-centered communication is, but they do allow a deeper level of coaching to take place. Some coaches like to schedule routine weekly audio or video check-ins with athletes, while others prefer to schedule them as needed. In either case, it should be clear to athletes what they are entitled to.

Informal communication by email, text, or phone is entirely a matter of individual discretion for coaches. If you prize your privacy, and your fees are below premium level, you may choose not to give out your mobile phone number to clients. Allowing athletes to call or text only in urgent situations is a policy that suits some coaches who are less comfortable granting athletes access to open communication. But if you enjoy open interaction with athletes, and you believe you do your best work when athletes are able to reach out to you spontaneously, if only to text you a photo of the snazzy new running shoes they just bought, then go right ahead and make this type of informal communication part of your system.

Rarely do athletes abuse the privilege of open access to their coach. Even if your rules for communication are lax, articulating them clearly in the process of onboarding new clients will further minimize this risk. More often, though, athletes aren't communicative enough with their coach. This typically happens either because they are time-crunched or they have a misplaced fear of "bothering" their coach. In such cases, let the athlete know you need more communication from them to do your job effectively. Identify the impediment and work with the athlete to develop a system that meets the needs of both parties.

Workflow

Online coaching is not a nine-to-five gig, but in order to do the job properly you must adhere to some kind of routine. After all, most athletes have consistent life schedules. If you don't sync your routine with theirs to some degree, you'll be like two ships passing in the night. Also, you'll be more efficient with your time if you get into the habit of performing certain tasks on particular days or at designated times during the day.

The specifics don't matter much. There's no universal optimal routine that every successful endurance coach must adhere to. What does matter is that the routine you come up with fits your lifestyle and your athletes' needs, and that it remains consistent, hence predictable for your athletes. Following is an example of a weekly work schedule:

MONDAY	Athlete calls
TUESDAY	Content development (e.g., recording video tips)
WEDNESDAY	Continuing education (e.g., catching up on sports science research)
THURSDAY	Planning next week's training
FRIDAY	Individualized athlete attention (e.g., pep talks for athletes with weekend races)
SATURDAY	Day off (coach's big training day)
SUNDAY	Analyzing athletes' training for the week completed

There aren't many coaches who set aside a single day each week to focus on a unique task, as in this example, but it is an option. Another option is assigning a primary task to each day while also tackling one or two secondary tasks. Alternatively, you might choose to spread your most time-consuming tasks across the week (for example, scheduling one athlete call or planning one athlete's training each weekday). If there are particular tasks you perform daily, you'll want to assign specific times to these as well. For example:

7:00 AM	Review each athlete's planned training for the day
10:00 AM	Create/post social media
9:00 PM	Review athletes' completed training

Roster Management

How will you recruit new clients? What is the maximum number of athletes you are comfortable coaching at one time? How will you handle offboarding clients? These are roster management questions and a big part of the business of coaching.

The first of these questions is also a marketing question, a topic we'll address in the next section. As for roster size, one thing that makes endurance coaching different from many other services is that the goal is not to acquire as many customers as possible. A coach can only take on so many athletes before the quality of their service begins to suffer. As a coach of integrity, you must never exceed your personal limit. The specific number varies from coach to coach depending on how many hours per week they're willing to work, how much individualized attention they can give to athletes, and their multitasking ability. You can either set a cap on your roster size that feels right and add athletes until you reach it, or you can add athletes one by one until you feel you've reached your limit and cap your roster there. Resist any temptation you might experience to go beyond your limit. The extra income isn't worth the sacrifice in quality of service.

Coaching also differs from other service professions with respect to the primary motivation for retaining clients. Whereas other service providers want to retain clients simply because long-term clients equal steady money, coaches want to hold on to their athletes because the better they get to know an athlete, the better they can coach them. For this reason, open-ended partnerships are the norm in endurance coaching. Yet all such partnerships end eventually, so it's best for coaches to be strategic in their handling of this reality to ensure that separation occurs at the right time and with minimal awkwardness.

One way to do this is to share your policy on separation with each athlete during the onboarding process. Explain that while you hope to work with them for a long time, they should feel comfortable moving on from you at any time and for any reason, and they should not worry about hurting your feelings or harming you financially. By the same token, you should reserve the right to terminate the partnership if you feel you are no longer able to coach the athlete effectively.

You can further reduce awkwardness around separating from clients by instituting a policy of formally revisiting the question of whether to continue working together after each completed training cycle. The idea here is not to place an artificial term limit on the partnership. It is to make both parties feel comfortable communicating their desire to move on when the time comes, and it reduces the likelihood of either party being caught off-guard when the other party broaches the subject.

Marketing

For better or worse, marketing is a huge part of the formula for success in online coaching. You could be the best coach in the world and still struggle to survive in the business if you fail to put sustained energy into letting athletes know you exist and setting yourself apart from other coaches in the marketplace. At the most basic level, there are two types of marketing you can do: offline and online. Offline marketing efforts entail hosting in-person workouts that are open to all athletes, offering educational clinics, and placing flyers in local stores that cater to athletes. Such efforts have limited reach, however, and make more sense for coaches pursuing the inherently local team/club model. Online marketing is where it's really at for coaches who work remotely. The three main online marketing tools used by successful coaches are content marketing, advertising, and search engine optimization.

Content Marketing

The Oxford Dictionary defines *content marketing* as "a type of marketing that involves the creation and sharing of online material (such as videos, blogs, and social media posts) that does not explicitly promote a brand but is intended to stimulate interest in its products or services." Of the many specific forms of content marketing that exist, endurance coaches typically have found the most success with social media, video, podcasting, blogging, and email marketing.

SOCIAL MEDIA

Social media offers the greatest return on investment for coaches seeking to market themselves, but only when it's done right. Here are some basic tips for doing it right:

Choose your platform(s) carefully. It is possible to recruit clients effectively on a variety of social media platforms, and each has its own advantages and disadvantages. Facebook is home to many large athlete groups (including 80/20 Endurance groups). You can use these groups to build your reputation and recruit clients just by chiming in with helpful advice and thoughtful answers to questions from other members. Instagram is advantageous to coaches with a creative flair and a knack for producing compelling visual content. Twitter's more casual nature makes it a good place to market yourself in a way that doesn't look like marketing. And there's no better place than TikTok to reach younger athletes.

Decide what your "thing" is. To rise above the chatter on social media, the content you share needs to be consistent in style and substance and be representative of your authentic self. In other words, you need to have a "thing." Options include highlighting the achievements of your athletes, offering commentary on hot topics in your sport, sharing your own athletic journey, focusing on inspirational messaging, and providing practical tips that aren't the same old thing. The simpler and more coherent your online coaching identity is, the stronger the impression you will make on athletes.

Interact and build relationships. Posting content is only half of what it takes to market yourself effectively on social media. Interacting and building relationships is the other half. Start by following key influencers in your space, as well as your own most loyal followers. Reply to comments and questions athletes leave on your posts and leave comments and questions on content posted by key influencers with whom you wish to build relationships. Establishing a strong social media presence takes time, but it's possible to reach a point where it begins to expand by its own momentum. Working hard to interact and build relationships is useful in getting to that point.

VIDEO

Technology has reached a level where any coach with a quality smartphone and an artist's eye can create and share compelling video content that promotes their brand and business. A number of endurance coaches have found success through this marketing vehicle by producing and releasing a steady drip of short videos that deliver practical tips for athletes. The keys to standing out from the crowd in this medium are quality and consistency. If you're going to do it, do it right. Take the time to create well-scripted, visually-appealing videos that provide actionable information in a concise and empathetic way. Release new videos frequently (at least once every week) on a fixed schedule that becomes habit-forming for viewers.

Of course, it's not enough simply to create good videos. You also need to make sure they're seen. Most coaches do this through social media, using this forum primarily as a vehicle for video content marketing. Others use video platforms such as YouTube or Vimeo as an alternative (or supplement) to their social media efforts. These platforms are a good option if you plan to create longer videos with high production value or host virtual events for athletes.

PODCASTS

The rise of podcasting has been a powerful democratizing force in auditory media. Creating a podcast is something almost anyone can do with minimal financial risk or technical know-how. For endurance coaches, hosting a podcast can be an effective way to build a reputation and recruit clients. Be forewarned, however: Most coaches who have taken this step will tell you the process was harder than they thought it would be. The tasks involved, such as creating a website for your show, editing interviews, scripting introductions, composing show notes, and booking guests, are more time-consuming than many newbies expect.

A good first step is to listen to existing endurance podcasts. Take note of things you like and wish to replicate in your own. Next, pick the brains of one or more podcast hosts. If you don't know any such individuals personally, try reaching out to the hosts of smaller shows you like. You might get the cold shoulder from some, but if you're persistent, you will eventually find one or more who are willing to share their knowledge and experience with you. Ask how they got started, what they did right, what their mistakes were, and what they would do differently if given a second chance, knowing what they know now. Among the biggest decisions you will need to make are which hosting platforms to use, whether to edit interviews yourself or hire a professional sound editor, how to distribute your show, and who you want as guests. In addition to talking directly with experienced podcasters, you can obtain guidance on these and other decisions through various podcasting primers findable on the internet through a simple Google search.

As with your other marketing efforts, take the long view in building your podcast. You can't expect your offering to make a meaningful impact on your coaching career in the first month or two. But if you remain patient, put in the work, and maintain high quality standards, the effort can pay off over time, as any successful podcaster will attest.

BLOGGING/EMAIL MARKETING

People have been forecasting the demise of the written word for decades, but it remains alive and well here in the twenty-first century. We may be biased by the fact that 80/20 Endurance was cofounded by a successful author, but we believe that text-based forms of content marketing—particularly blogging and email marketing—can be highly effective business development tools for endurance coaches. Blogging, of course, entails posting articles you've written on a website you control (such as your coaching website) or on a public forum such as Medium or LinkedIn, while email marketing entails sending out e-newsletters or similar materials on a regular schedule to a list of subscribers you maintain.

These tools will only succeed for you, however, if you enjoy and have a knack for writing. There's a saying in the literary arts: "Writers write." If you're one of those people who truly need to express themselves through writing, then you might as well put this skill to use to help your coaching business. As with all of the other forms of content marketing we've discussed, succeeding with blogging or email marketing requires strategy, consistency, patience, and high standards for quality. Make use of content marketing services such as MailChimp to work toward your goals.

Advertising/Search Engine Optimization

In the contemporary media environment, there are myriad ways to advertise, ranging from 30-second spots on national television to virtual goodie bag promotional offers. While a majority of the advertising vehicles available to endurance coaches have little or no relevance to their interests, a few do.

Among these is search engine optimization (SEO), an esoteric science comprising various tricks designed to increase website traffic by exploiting the rules that search engines use to rank the results of keyword searches, such as "cycling coach." Although SEO doesn't qualify as advertising in the strictest sense, it achieves the same result as paying Google to have your website ranked higher in search results, which is a form of advertising.

If you manage your own website, you can improve your SEO to a degree by taking some time to learn and apply these tricks. Most freelance professional web designers have some knowledge of the ins and outs of SEO, so if you choose to outsource the design and management of your website, look for a freelancer who is savvy about SEO. There are also contractors who focus exclusively on optimizing content for search. Be aware, however, that this sector is filled with charlatans who charge a lot of money and offer little value in return. The happiest clients are typically those who choose an SEO specialist on the basis of a referral from a trusted individual.

Another cost-effective (often free) way to advertise your coaching services is to create listings on online directories. Most organizations (including 80/20 Endurance) that offer coaching certifications provide such listings as a perk for getting certified. Take full advantage of any and all opportunities of this kind. Similarly, the various online platforms that are available to endurance coaches have directories of their own. Some of these are two-tiered, providing a basic listing with a paid coaching account and a more prominent listing—or even a lead-generating service—for an additional fee. TrainingPeaks's Coach Match program is one example.

A variety of other entities, including some endurance media organizations, offer "Find a Coach" services. Among these is slowtwitch.com, which has a popular directory of North American triathlon coaches. Not every directory out there is worth joining, but for those that are, put your best foot forward. Create a listing that stands apart with a high-quality portrait or action photo of you and a concise and engaging sales pitch.

Paid online advertising is not often used to market independent coaching services. The reason is that, although Facebook and other major platforms allow advertisers to target specific demographics (such as runners), the decision to hire a coach is made far less frequently than the decision to, say, buy a new pair of running shoes. The conversion rate is very low with this type of outreach. That being said, there are low-risk ways of experimenting with online advertising. One is using cookies on your website to mark individual visitors and target those athletes with advertising. When you reach a point where your website is receiving decent traffic, and you want to turn more of that attention into revenue, you might consider giving paid advertising a try. Think it through, though, and give it a proper chance. Decide how much money you're willing to risk on the experiment, develop an appealing and professional ad campaign, study the results, tweak your strategy based on what you learn, and try again and again until you've either succeeded or maxed out your budget without enough return to justify further outlays.

A FINAL NOTE

Building a coaching business is hard work, but it isn't any harder than coaching itself. It only seems harder to those who enjoy the coaching part more than they enjoy the business part. Self-promotion doesn't come naturally to a lot of endurance coaches, which can lead to discouragement with the process of building a successful coaching business. If you become discouraged at any point in this journey, keep in mind that you're not just trying to get your name out there for the sake of being known. You're trying to get your name out there because somewhere out there is an athlete whose life will be profoundly impacted for the better if and when you do reach them.

Sample Athlete Intake Questionnaire

1. Why are you interested in having me coach you?

2. When would you like to start?

3. What is your current priority goal?

4. What are your immediate and long-term athletic goals (if different from the above)?

5. Please estimate your finish time for each of the following single-sport races if you were to do them today (be honest!):

   1500m pool swim:
   40K cycling time trial (flat):
   10K run (flat):

6. Describe your recent training (typical week). Be as concrete/quantitative as possible (e.g., average weekly swim, bike, run frequency and distance).

7. What is the longest swim, longest bike ride, and longest run you've done in the last three weeks?

8. How many workouts per week are you comfortable doing?

9. What is the best day of the week for your longest session(s)?

10. Are there any specific days of the week when you cannot or prefer not to train?

11. Use the table below to share your current and/or preferred weekly workout routine.

	MON	TUE	WED	THU	FRI	SAT	SUN
A.M.							
P.M.							

12. Would you like me to include strength workouts in your schedule? If so, which specific days of the week are best for these?

13. Please identify any other training preferences you have and would like to maintain throughout this training plan (e.g., a Saturday masters swim class).

14. Where do you typically run (paved streets, dirt trails, running track, treadmill)?

15. Do you have convenient access to hills to cycle/run on?

16. Are you able to cycle indoors? If so, how often do you normally do so?

17. Which devices do you use to record your workouts?

18. Please describe your history of overuse injuries.

19. Is there anything else you would like me to know?

Glossary

acute training load (ATL): A rolling average of training stress imposed on the athlete over the past several days. It is commonly used as a measure of fatigue.

acyclic periodization: Training at a high but sustainable baseline level that allows athletes to sharpen up quickly for races and then return to baseline after a short recovery period.

anaerobic capacity: The maximum rate at which an athlete's body is able to generate energy for muscle work without the aid of oxygen.

block periodization: Multiweek blocks of training that feature a lot of volume and little or no work at higher intensities.

cardiac drift: A phenomenon whereby the athlete's heart rate slowly increases during a long workout done at steady pace or power. It is caused by a combination of dehydration and loss of mechanical efficiency resulting from fatigue.

chronic training load (CTL): A rolling average of training stress imposed on the athlete over the past few weeks. It is commonly used as a measure of fitness.

corrective exercises: Exercises used to strengthen smaller muscles responsible for stabilizing joints during sports movements.

descriptive data: Information that describes what happened during the workout in pertinent, reliable terms.

diagnostic data: Information that describes why something happened in a workout.

dynamic stretches: Moving a joint repeatedly through a full range of motion, which over time reduces internal resistance, allowing similar movements to be performed more comfortably and efficiently.

explosive movements: Also known as ballistic exercises, these movements are strength exercises performed at high speed.

first ventilatory threshold (VT$_1$): The lower of two intensities at which an athlete's breathing rate spikes.

functional correlates: A performance standard or other practical limit that corresponds to a particular physiological threshold.

functional strength exercises: Exercises that simulate and strengthen sport-specific actions.

functional threshold power (FTP): The highest power a cyclist can sustain for one hour, or the upper limit of Zone 3 in the 80/20 Endurance intensity scale.

heart rate variability (HRV): A biometric indicator of how the body is responding to the load.

heavy lifts: Strength exercises involving multiple muscle groups and movement against high levels of resistance.

individualization: The process of tailoring training to the unique needs of the athlete, which are continuously changing.

intensity: How hard an athlete is working relative to their limit.

isometric exercises: Static muscle contractions.

lactate threshold (LT): The exercise intensity at which lactate, an intermediate product of aerobic metabolism, begins to accumulate rapidly in the bloodstream. The average trained endurance athlete is able to sustain this intensity for about 60 minutes.

linear macrocyle: A period of training that is made up of distinct phases, each emphasizing a specific component of fitness.

load: How much weight or resistance is used for a given strength exercise and for how long.

load density: A comparison of total training time to frequency, where less frequency creates more training load density.

load orientation: The specific focus of a workout or block of workouts.

macrocycle: A period of training that is focused on preparing the athlete for a single peak performance.

mental fitness: The ability to make the best of a bad situation.

mesocycle (or step cycle): The primary instrument by which coaches apply the principle of progression in planning an athlete's training. A mesocycle consists of two to three microcycles with incrementally increasing loads followed by a recovery microcycle with reduced load.

microcycle: Seven to ten days of relatively fixed structure in which workouts of different activity types, intensities, and stress levels are spread out as much as possible.

mobility: The ability to perform athletic movements without restriction.

motivational interview: A collaborative, client-centered approach to help athletes develop mental fitness.

myofascial release: Self-massage using implements such as foam rollers, the purpose of which is to enhance muscle tissue pliability.

nonlinear macrocycle: The distinct phases that characterize linear periodization are replaced with something more organic and fluid.

overreaching: Training at a level that is not sustainable for the athlete. Overreaching can be either functional or nonfunctional. *Functional overreaching* results in fitness improvement if it is not too extreme or sustained too long. *Nonfunctional overreaching* occurs when the athlete trains beyond their body's capacity to adapt beneficially.

perceived effort (or Rate of Perceived Exertion, RPE): An athlete's internal sense of how hard they are working.

periodization: The art of sequencing workouts to achieve specific training objectives.

predictive data: Supplies information about what is likely to happen in the future— i.e., race readiness.

prescriptive data: Supplies information about how to make a desired outcome happen.

proprioceptive cues: Images, kinesthetic prompts, and other mental tools that help an athlete execute correct technique.

proprioceptive exercises: Exercises that challenge the athlete's ability to maintain stability while moving.

reality therapy: A psychotherapeutic method developed to help people make responsible decisions that are consistent with their values and grounded in a clear understanding of reality.

second ventilatory threshold (VT$_2$): Intensity that falls between 91 and 93 percent of maximum heart rate for the majority of athletes.

static stretches: Holding a muscle in a stretched position to increase passive range of motion.

steady state workout: A less intense workout comprising a single, prolonged effort in Zone X.

sweet spot: The upper limit of the body's capacity to absorb and adapt to training.

tempo workout: A moderate-intensity workout with one or more extended efforts at or near lactate threshold, or the upper limit of Zone 3.

training load: A way of measuring how hard an athlete is training by factoring together training volume and training intensity.

training monotony: Quantifies the variation in session duration within a week of training.

training stress score (TSS): A measure of physiological stress imposed on the athlete by an individual workout, which is calculated by factoring together the duration and the intensity of the session.

ultrarealist: An athlete who is able to make the best of a bad situation by accepting, embracing, and addressing problems that arise.

VO$_2$max: Corresponds to an effort that the average trained athlete can sustain for roughly six minutes.

volume: The overall amount of training an athlete is doing, measured in time or distance, usually on a weekly basis.

Resources

Introduction

Fitzgerald, Matt. *80/20 Running: Run Stronger and Race Faster by Training Slower*. New York: Berkley, 2004.

Fitzgerald, Matt, and David Warden. *80/20 Triathlon: Discover the Breakthrough Elite Training Formula for Ultimate Fitness and Performance at All Levels*. Boston: Da Capo, 2018.

Seiler, Stephen. "What Is Best Practice for Training Intensity and Duration Distribution in Endurance Athletes?" *Internal Journal of Sports Physiology and Performance*. 2010 Sept. 5(3):276–91.

Seiler, Stephen. "How 'Normal' People Can Train Like the World's Best Endurance Athletes." YouTube video, 17:39. Posted by TedX, December 2, 2019.

Chapter 1

Baker, Joe. *The Tyranny of Talent: How It Compels and Limits Athletic Achievement . . . And Why You Should Ignore It*. Montreal: Aberrant, 2022.

Cheung, Stephen. *Advanced Environmental Exercise Physiology*. Champaign: Human Kinetics, 2021.

Fast Talk Laboratories. https://www.fasttalklabs.com

Gareth Sandford (@Gareth_Sandford). https://twitter.com/Gareth_Sandford

Skiba, Philip. *Scientific Training for Endurance Athletes*. Park Ridge: PhysFarm, 2021.

Chapter 2

Fitzgerald, Matt. "Intensity Guidelines for Cycling." 80/20 Endurance. https://www.8020endurance.com/intensity-guidelines-for-cycling/

Fitzgerald, Matt. "Intensity Guidelines for Running." 80/20 Endurance. https://www.8020endurance.com/intensity-guidelines-for-8020-running/

Fitzgerald, Matt and David Warden. "Intensity Guidelines for Triathlon." 80/20 Endurance. https://www.8020endurance.com/intensity-guidelines-for-8020-triathlon/

Chapter 3

Fitzgerald, Matt. "All About (Intensity) Balance." 80/20 Endurance. https://www.8020endurance.com/allaboutintensitybalance/

Stöggl, Thomas L., and Billy Sperlich. "The Training Intensity Distribution Among Well-Trained and Elite Endurance Athletes." *Frontiers in Physiology* 2015 Oct. 27, 6(295).

Chapter 4

Mujika, Iñigo. "Quantification of Training and Competition Loads in Endurance Sports: Methods and Applications." *International Journal of Sports Physiology and Performance* 2017, 12 Suppl 2(2017):S29-S217.

Mujika, Iñigo, and Sabino Padilla. "Scientific Bases for Precompetition Tapering Strategies." *Medicine & Science in Sports and Exercise*, 2003 Jul., 35(7):1182–1187.

Warden, David. "Understanding and Adjusting Your Performance Management Chart." 80/20 Endurance. https://www.8020endurance.com/performance-management-chart-is-lying-to-you/

Chapter 5

Bompa, Tudor, and Carlo Buzzichelli. *Periodization: Theory and Methodology of Training, 6th Ed.* Champaign: Human Kinetics, 2018.

Kenneally, Mark, Arturo Casado, Jordan Santos-Concejero. "The Effect of Periodization and Training Intensity Distribution on Middle- and Long-Distance Running Performance: A Systematic Review." *International Journal of Sports Physiology and Performance*, 2018 Oct. 1, 13(9):1114–1121.

Mølmen, Knut Sindre, Sjur Johansen Øfsteng, Bent R. Rønnestad. "Block Periodization of Endurance Training: A Systematic Review and Meta-Analysis." *Open Access Journal of Sports Medicine*, 2019 Oct. 17, 10:145–160.

Chapter 6

Epstein, David. *Range: Why Generalists Triumph in a Specialized World.* New York: Riverhead, 2019.

Houtmeyers, Kobe C., Arne Jaspers, Pedro Figueiredo. "Managing the Training Process in Elite Sports: From Descriptive to Prescriptive Data Analytics." *International Journal of Sports Physiology and Performance*, 2021 Nov. 1, 16(11):1719–1723.

Lehman, Greg. "Reconciling Biomechanics with Pain Science." Online Course. http://www.greglehman.ca/new-page-1

Paragon Athletics. https://paragonathletics.com

Walker, Brad. *The Anatomy of Sports Injuries: Your Illustrated Guide to Prevention, Diagnosis, and Treatment.* Berkeley: North Atlantic, 2018.

Chapter 7

Dan Daly (dandaly). https://www.instagram.com/dandaly/

Flynn, Michael G., Kathy K. Carroll, Heather L. Hall, Barbara A. Bushman, Per Gunner Brolinson, Carol A. Weideman. "Cross Training: Indices of Training Stress and Performance." *Medicine & Science in Sports & Exercise.* 1998 Feb. 30(2):294–300.

Hall, Gary, and Devin Murphy. *Fundamentals of Fast Swimming: How to Improve Your Swim Technique.* Bowker: New Providence, 2020.

House, Steve, Scott Johnston, and Killian Jornet. *Training for the Uphill Athlete: A Manual for Mountain Runners and Ski Mountaineers.* Ventura: Patagonia, 2019.

Löw Tide Böyz podcast. https://lowtideboyz.com

McLeod, Ian. *Swimming Anatomy.* Champaign: Human Kinetics, 2009.

Nolte, Volker, and Wolfgang Fritsch. *Master Rowing: Training for Technique, Fitness, and Competition.* Aachen: Meyer & Meyer, 2021.

Overlier, Hanne, and Sindre Bergan. *Cross Country Skiing: The Norwegian Way,* 2nd Ed. Total Health: Oslo, 2019.

Yeager, Selene. *Gravel! The Ultimate Guide to the Gear, Training, and Grit You Need to Crush It.* New York: Hearst, 2019.

Chapter 8

Blagrove, Richard. *Strength and Conditioning for Endurance Running.* Ramsbury: Crowood, 2015.

Human Performance Education. http://www.andygalpin.com

LEO Training podcast. https://leotraining.libsyn.com

National Strength & Conditioning Association. *Essentials of Strength Training and Conditioning.* Champaign: Human Kinetics, 2015.

National Strength & Conditioning Association. *Exercise Technique Manual for Resistance Training.* Champaign: Human Kinetics, 2016.

Sports Therapy Association podcast. https://www.youtube.com/c/sportstherapyassociation

Strength for Endurance podcast. https://www.strengthforendurance.com/podcast

Strengthrunning.com. https://strengthrunning.com

Chapter 9

Fitzgerald, Matt. *On Pace: Discover How to Run at Your Real Limit in Every Race*. Lehi: 80/20, 2022.

Jeukendrup, Asker, and Michael Gleeson. *Sport Nutrition*. Champaign: Human Kinetics, 2018. Aachen: Meyer & Meyer, 2021.

My Sports Science. https://www.mysportscience.com

Viribay, Aitor. "The Six Phases of Training the Gut: From 0 to 120 g/hr Carbohydrates." *Glut4 Science*, 2020 May 28. https://glut4science.com/publicaciones/entrenamiento-nutricional/training-the-gut-phases-from-0-to-120-g-h-carbohydrate/93

Wilson, Patrick. *The Athlete's Gut: The Inside Science of Digestion, Nutrition, and Stomach Distress*. Boulder: VeloPress, 2020.

Chapter 10

Bartholomew, Brett. *Conscious Coaching: The Art and Science of Building Buy-In*. CreateSpace, 2017.

Clifford, Dawn, and Laura Curtiss. *Motivational Interviewing in Nutrition and Fitness*. New York: Guilford, 2015.

Cranmer, Gregory. *Athlete Coaching: A Communication Perspective*. Bern: Peter Lang, 2019.

Fitzgerald, Matt. *The Comeback Quotient: A Get-Real Guide to Building Mental Fitness in Sport and Life*. Boulder: VeloPress, 2020.

Chapter 11

Huber, Jeffrey. *Applying Educational Psychology in Coaching Athletes*. Champaign: Human Kinetics, 2012.

Simon, Robert (editor). *The Ethics of Coaching Sports: Moral, Social, and Legal Issues*. London: Routledge, 2013.

Smith, Ronald. *Sport Psychology for Youth Coaches: Developing Champions in Sport and Life*. Lanham: Rowman & Littlefield, 2012.

Chapter 12

Introduction to Business for Endurance Coaches. Online course. https://university.trainingpeaks.com/introduction-to-business-for-endurance-coaches

About the Author

Matt Fitzgerald is an acclaimed endurance sports author, coach, and nutritionist. His many books include *The Comeback Quotient*, *80/20 Running*, and *How to Run the Perfect Race*. Matt has also written for a number of leading sports and fitness publications, including *Runner's World* and *Triathlete*, and for popular websites such as outsideonline.com and nbcnews.com. He is cofounder of 80/20 Endurance, the world's premier endurance sports training brand. He also codirects the Coaches of Color Initiative, a non-profit program that seeks to improve diversity in endurance coaching. A lifelong endurance athlete, Matt speaks frequently at events throughout the United States and internationally.